Ethical Practice in
Operational
Psychology

Ethical Practice in Operational Psychology

MILITARY AND NATIONAL INTELLIGENCE APPLICATIONS

Edited by Carrie H. Kennedy
and Thomas J. Williams

American Psychological Association • Washington, DC

Published by
American Psychological Association
750 First Street, NE
Washington, DC 20002
www.apa.org

To order
APA Order Department
P.O. Box 92984
Washington, DC 20090-2984
Tel: (800) 374-2721; Direct: (202) 336-5510
Fax: (202) 336-5502; TDD/TTY: (202) 336-6123
Online: www.apa.org/pubs/books
E-mail: order@apa.org

In the U.K., Europe, Africa, and the Middle East, copies may be ordered from
American Psychological Association
3 Henrietta Street
Covent Garden, London
WC2E 8LU England

Typeset in Goudy by Circle Graphics, Inc., Columbia, MD

Printer: Maple-Vail Book Manufacturing Group, York, PA
Cover Designer: Mercury Publishing Services, Rockville, MD

The opinions and statements published are the responsibility of the authors, and such opinions and statements do not necessarily represent the policies of the American Psychological Association.

Library of Congress Cataloging-in-Publication Data

Ethical practice in operational psychology : military and national intelligence applications / edited by Carrie H. Kennedy and Thomas J. Williams.
   p. cm.
Includes bibliographical references and index.
ISBN-13: 978-1-4338-0711-4
ISBN-10: 1-4338-0711-4
 1. Operational psychology—Moral and ethical aspects. 2. Operational psychologists—Professional ethics. 3. Military interrogation—Moral and ethical aspects. 4. Police questioning—Moral and ethical aspects. 5. Intelligence service—Moral and ethical aspects. 6. Terrorism—Prevention—Moral and ethical aspects. I. Williams, Thomas J. II. Kennedy, Carrie H. III. American Psychological Association

 BF636.3.E84 2011
 174'.915—dc22
                            2009022513

British Library Cataloguing-in-Publication Data

A CIP record is available from the British Library.

Printed in the United States of America
First Edition

To my great uncle
Machinist Mate 2nd Class (U. S. Navy)
Wyllys C. Smith.
1916–2008
Carrie H. Kennedy

In memoriam to my father and mother
Charles E. and Mary Lea Williams;
for life, for strength, and for perspective . . .
Thomas J. Williams

The views expressed in this publication are those of the authors and do not reflect the official policy or position of the Department of the Army, Department of the Air Force, Department of the Navy, Department of Defense, the United States Government, or any other agency for which the authors are employed. Further, such opinions and statements do not represent the official policies, standards, guidelines, or ethical mandates of the American Psychological Association (APA), the APA Ethics Committee, the APA Ethics Office, or any other APA governance group or staff. Statements made in this book neither add to nor reduce requirements of the APA "Ethical Principles of Psychologists and Code of Conduct" (APA, 2010),[1] hereinafter referred to as the APA Ethics Code or the Ethics Code, nor can they be viewed as a definitive source of the meaning of the Ethics Code standards or their application to particular situations. Each ethics committee or other relevant body must interpret and apply the Ethics Code as it believes proper, given all the circumstances of each particular situation. Any information in this book involving legal and ethical issues should not be used as a substitute for obtaining personal legal and/or ethical advice and consultation prior to making decisions regarding individual circumstances.

[1]American Psychological Association. (2010). *Ethical principles of psychologists and code of conduct.* (*2002, Amended June 1, 2010*). Retrieved from http://www.apa.org/ethics/code/index.aspx

CONTENTS

CONTRIBUTORS

Colonel L. Morgan Banks, PhD, U.S. Army Special Operations Command, Fort Bragg, NC

Randy Borum, PhD, University of South Florida, Tampa

Colonel Debra Dunivin, PhD, ABPP, Walter Reed Army Medical Center, Washington, DC

Robert Fein, PhD, U.S. Department of Defense, Arlington, VA

Michael G. Gelles, PsyD, ABPP, Washington, DC

Sally Harvey, PhD, 902nd Military Intelligence Group, Fort Meade, MD

Carrie H. Kennedy, PhD, ABPP, Pensacola, FL

Kirk Kennedy, PhD, U.S. Department of Defense, Arlington, VA

Carla Long, PhD, U.S. Department of Defense, Fort Belvoir, VA

Russell Palarea, PhD, Staff Operational Psychologist, Naval Criminal Investigative Service, Alexandria, VA

James Picano, PhD, U.S. Army Reserve, Suisun, CA

Robert Roland, PhD, U.S. Department of Defense, Fort Belvoir, VA

Lieutenant Colonel Mark A. Staal, PhD, Joint Special Operations Command, Fort Bragg, NC

Lieutenant Colonel James A. Stephenson, PsyD, ABPP, Moody Air Force Base, Valdosta, GA

Thomas J. Williams, PhD, Carlisle, PA

James Young, PhD, 1st Special Operations Wing, Hurlburt Field, FL

ACKNOWLEDGMENTS

In the late 1990s, a number of psychologists who supported national security programs would meet monthly to collaboratively discuss program and research initiatives. The need for psychologists to remain focused on a professional and ethical practice of psychology in support of national security operations was a frequent topic of those meetings. Thus, the meetings often served as professional peer consultations in a practice domain that has come to be known as operational psychology. Various potential and real ethical conflicts related to the practice of psychology in support of national security missions were addressed in those meetings. Many of those discussions serve as the foundational impetus for this book. It also goes without saying that the dramatic increase in relevance and practice of operational psychologists in a post-9/11 world reinforces the need to bring that foundation into a structure of practice. This volume is intended to help frame that structure and guide those operational psychologists, who now face a vast array of complex challenges around the world.

Publishing a book is always a challenge. This book proved to be more so than usual given the ongoing debate about psychologists consulting to interrogations, the emotional reactions regarding this topic, and the real-world demands (e.g., deployments) on the contributors. In addition, the national security policies that provide a legal foundation and that serve to both inform and anchor ethical considerations have provided an additional dynamic and challenge. Consequently, the debate about the proper role for psychologists within this context continues. It is our intention that this volume provide firsthand knowledge about the key areas of operational psychological practice and the ethical analysis needed to operate in this relatively uncharted territory.

In this context, we want to acknowledge a small number of individuals who made this book possible. First is the American Psychological Association editorial staff; our original editor, Lansing Hayes, advocated for its publication, and Susan Reynolds, Genevieve Gill, Judy Nemes, and Dan Brachtesende saw it through.

We are in constant debt to our many mentors: Admiral Mike Mittelman has been a continuous source of inspiration over the years; Dr. Jack Smith and Colonel Sean Murphy have been staunch advocates for the publication of scholarly material on psychologists and their roles in the war; Commander Andy Davidson has been the consummate role model; and Brad Johnson, Captain Tony McDonald, and Eric Zillmer have provided endless sound advice and constructive feedback. We must also recognize Major General Charles Cleveland for his innovative and supportive role. As an operational commander, his willingness to consider the contributions of operational psychologists in a direct support role helped to establish the relevance and responsiveness of this emerging area of expertise. Special recognition is due to Colonel Morgan Banks, Dr. Mike Gelles, Colonel (retired) Bob Roland, and Colonel Jim Picano, all of whom are contributors to this volume. Perhaps no one has worked harder and more strategically than Morgan Banks to preserve the delicate balance between many complex national security interests and the ethical practice of psychology. Mike Gelles is truly a legend in his own time and is the personification of how psychologists really can get this right. Bob Roland and Jim Picano are tireless and innovative thinkers who have supported some of the most important programs and processes, and both serve as role models for how to blend the science and practice of psychology.

We also must acknowledge and express our heartfelt appreciation to several past presidents of the American Psychological Association: in particular, Diane Halpern, Ron Levant, Gerald Koocher, and Sharon Brehm. They have helped guide the discussion about psychologists in support of national security programs in terms of both ethics and practice. In doing so, they demonstrated the value of leaders who establish and maintain the profession as a uniting and innovative force that serves as a catalyst for and leading advocate for the practice of psychology with national security policymakers. There is no doubt about the benefit of allowing psychologists to serve as principal leaders in the facilitation and resolution of many of the personal, societal, and global challenges Americans now confront and to promote human rights, health, well-being, and dignity. These are the principles that help guide the American Psychological Association. A close reading of the chapters contained within this volume will reveal that operational psychologists help maintain and reinforce those principles.

Finally and foremost we want to recognize our chapter authors. Many of the authors of this volume have had to reconcile the frequently competing challenges that confront operational psychologists when organizational demands and professional ethics are not in perfect alignment. We commend our authors for their frank accounts of their operational positions and how ethical issues are managed in their environments. They have been unrelenting in their efforts to seek out an ethical practice of psychology even as they have sacrificed their safety, their comfort, and time with their family as they have answered the call to support our national security interests. In the spirit of extraparadigmatic thinking (viz., Thomas Kuhn) they have braved the social dimension of science and practice to explore, explain, and advance the ethics of operational psychology.

Ethical Practice in
Operational
Psychology

1

OPERATIONAL PSYCHOLOGY ETHICS: ADDRESSING EVOLVING DILEMMAS

CARRIE H. KENNEDY AND THOMAS J. WILLIAMS

Operational psychology is an evolving psychology specialty that provides a conceptual framework for the varied roles and responsibilities of military and government psychologists, in support of national security, public safety, and corrections. The continuously expanding use of operational psychologists in support of police activities and military operations, as in wars over the past century (see, e.g., Boring, 1945; McGuire, 1990; Office of Strategic Services [OSS], 1948; Yerkes, 1918, 1919; Zeidner & Drucker, 1988), has expanded the scope and functions of psychologists. This expansion of roles includes assessment, selection, certification, training, profiling, and other professional activities, including consultation to interrogations and counterintelligence operations. These increasing roles and responsibilities, which draw on the expertise of psychologists, have not been without critics (e.g., Summers, 2007). Both the expanded roles and the criticisms have served as an important impetus to more clearly and explicitly define the field and provide an ethical framework within which operational psychologists can perform their professional duties.

The views expressed in this article are those of the authors and do not reflect the official policy or position of the U.S. Department of the Army, U.S. Department of the Navy, U.S. Department of Defense, or the U.S. Government.

Williams, Picano, Roland, and Banks, (2006) defined operational psychology as

> actions by military psychologists that support the employment and/or sustainment of military forces to attain strategic goals in a theater of war or theater of operations by leveraging and applying their psychological expertise in helping to identify enemy capabilities, personalities, and intentions; facilitating and supporting intelligence operations; designing and implementing assessment and selection programs in support of special populations and high-risk missions; and providing an operationally focused level of mental health support. (pp. 194–195)

Staal and Stephenson (2006) offered a more restrictive scope of practice, which defined operational psychology as "the use of psychological principles and skills to improve a commander's decision making as it pertains to conducting combat and/or related operations," (p. 271) and they suggested that this field be viewed as an intelligence rather than a medical function. These definitions denote an applied military use specifically, though it is evident that operational psychology has emerged equally outside of the military within law enforcement and intelligence communities (e.g., OSS, 1948; Rowe, Gelles, & Palarea, 2006).

To provide a more inclusive definition of this emerging field, in this book, we provide an updated definition of operational psychology as *the application of the science and profession of psychology to the operational activities of law enforcement, national intelligence organizations, and national defense activities.* This revision recognizes that operational psychology has its origins in the development and application of psychological principles to the issues; roles; responsibilities; and questions of relevance to national security, national intelligence, and law enforcement activities. Operational psychology is clearly rooted in the clinical discipline of psychology, but professional activities may also depend on a developed expertise within other psychological specialties (e.g., social, cross-cultural, personality, police, political, learning and perception, individual and group differences, forensic psychology). Operational psychologists must also be interdisciplinary in their scope of activities, often drawing on such diverse disciplines as anthropology, sociology, military science, political science, and international law.

The practice area of operational psychology provides an emerging and critical role for psychologists who seek positions that support our national security interests in collaboration with military operations and intelligence and law enforcement agencies that advance those interests. Consequently, operational psychologists focus their practice, expertise, and research interests on contributing, as appropriate, to the operational art and science of integrating tactical, operational, and strategic national security objectives into applied activities. Their contributions, many of which are the focus of this volume, may range from helping a military commander enhance his or her understanding of the personality of an adversary to helping inform national policies regarding the science behind eliciting information. Government policies since the September 11, 2001, attacks on the United States have propelled the growth of operational psychology as a field. These policies have created a wide array of new roles and helped to fine-tune existing roles for those psychologists who consult to agencies and who work to provide operational support to military commanders and other law enforcement leaders.

In a special issue of *Military Psychology*, Williams and Johnson (2006) helped to frame the varied roles and responsibilities for operational psychologists who focus their services on national security issues in both military and government settings. These authors noted:

> Toward that end, operational psychologists must remain responsive and adaptive to the vigorous operational tempo and continuous challenge of serving a nation at war. Because of these often unique and challenging practice applications and environments, both military and other government agency psychologists increasingly face unique clinical concerns, practice challenges, and professional stressors. (p. 262)

Operational psychologists must be individuals who are able to grasp the often strategic nature of their activities and who are willing to share their expertise to operate within often austere and at times dangerous applied settings. The situations operational psychologists may find themselves in can be quite dynamic and, given that the field is emerging, with few role models. Operational psychologists must enter the field with solid core skills and a thorough grounding in the ethical foundation of psychology practice.

Psychologists working for national security organizations are finding themselves increasingly sought after to fill roles that are nontraditional for psychologists to provide operational support to a variety of agencies. They are expanding their expertise to counterespionage and counterterrorism efforts (Shumate & Borum, 2006) and are working to improve the effectiveness and safety of interrogation techniques. For decades, psychologists have been involved in hostage and crisis negotiation (see Rowe et al., 2006) and personnel selection for high-risk and high-demand occupations (e.g., Banks, 2006; OSS, 1948; Picano, Williams, & Roland, 2006). Operational psychologists currently work in a variety of settings that include intelligence agencies; Survival, Evasion, Resistance, and Escape (SERE) schools; special operations commands; and law enforcement agencies performing such tasks as behavioral profiling, interrogation or crisis negotiation consultation, threat assessment, repatriation of hostages and prisoners of war, and military special forces selection (Staal & Stephenson, 2006).

ROLES OF PSYCHOLOGISTS IN LAW ENFORCEMENT, INTELLIGENCE, AND MILITARY AGENCIES

Law enforcement, intelligence organizations, and the military employ large numbers of psychologists with varying academic backgrounds and training. Although there can be considerable overlap among their job functions, these individuals can be loosely grouped into research, clinical, and operational psychologists.

Research psychologists, who represent the gamut of psychological specialties with varying psychology-oriented training (e.g., industrial and organizational, experimental, cognitive), have been actively involved in applying psychological principles for the military since 1917. Around this time, 130 psychologists were made officers in U.S. Army. Interestingly, this number was also 40% of the membership of the American Psychological Association (APA) at that time (Zeidner & Drucker, 1988). The officers' primary area of focus initially was employment testing. The roles of research psychologists in government agencies have expanded dramatically over the years, however, to include increasing the efficacy of manned systems, deriving effective recruiting strategies, evaluating the psychological effects of combat and police shootings, optimizing and understanding the factors involved in the accuracy of eye witness testimony, optimizing training evolutions, increasing unit cohesion, threat risk assessment, and developing leaders (see, e.g., Coggins, Pynchon, & Dvoskin, 1998; Wells et al., 2000). Within national security agencies, some of these psychologists have become highly specialized. For example, U.S. Navy aerospace experimental psychologists have existed since 1941. Today these psychologists serve aviation personnel and commands and consult on airborne systems. Their primary areas of focus are human factors engineering, personnel assessment and selection, training development and evaluation, crew resource management, research, and development of new systems. These psychologists maintain flight status and routinely fly to maintain an adequate understanding of the specialized population that they serve.

Clinical psychologists are employed nationally in a wide variety of jobs in the fields of forensic psychology, neuropsychology, health psychology, child psychology, and other specialties. Increasingly, some may have prescription privileges. The primary responsibilities of these professionals are to directly evaluate and, with the exception of psychologists in a forensic role, provide psychological interventions as part of behavioral health care for individuals. Clinical psychologists assess and maintain the mental health of individuals and provide services in a doctor–patient model.

Operational psychologists typically are developed from the pool of clinical psychologists because operational psychologists require, as noted earlier, a comprehensive understanding of mental health conditions, personality dynamics, and assessment and evaluation procedures as well as of the U.S. Department of Defense (DoD) and national security laws and directives. However, it is important to note that other psychology specialty areas perform some of these functions. For example, the U.S. Navy's aerospace experimental psychologists (see the preceding mention), who generally have degrees oriented toward cognitive, research, or industrial and organizational psychology, perform some traditional operational psychology functions, such as developing and maintaining the assessment and selection procedures for officer aviation candidates for both the U.S. Navy and Marine Corps.

Operational psychologists perform a wide variety of functions, some of which overlap with research and clinical psychologists' traditional functions. Operational psychologists conduct research (e.g., stress-related research in mock prisoner-of-war training scenarios), work to improve employee quality and work product (e.g., assessment and selection), and at times perform evaluations that are clinical in nature (e.g., security clearance evaluations designed to assess the judgment and reliability of individuals for positions of trust). However, it is important to emphasize that although they often have clinical training, operational psychologists do not work in what many would consider a traditionally clinical role. That is, their primary focus is not on delivering health care. Rather, similar to forensic psychologists, their roles, responsibilities, and practice remain focused on those activities in which a sophisticated understanding of human nature helps achieve a vital protective function in support of national security and, by extension, society.

When defining the breadth of the field of operational psychology, psychologists hold mixed views as to whether the practice of clinical psychology in an operational environment (e.g., combat zone) is an element of the newer domain of operational psychology (see, e.g., Williams & Johnson, 2006). Although strict clinical services, even under fire, are not an element (Staal & Stephenson, 2006) and are probably more precisely termed *expeditionary psychology*, clinicians in these environments are at significant risk of being asked to perform operational psychology functions. Reasons for this range from simple proximity and the frequent misperception among nonmedical personnel that all psychologists can perform the same functions to the current significant shortage of military psychologists available for deployment. In addition, at times clinical roles may intersect with nonclinical issues pertaining to national security, such as when a detainee–patient provides information of intelligence value to a treating psychologist (Kennedy & Johnson, 2009). For these reasons, clinical psychologists who may deploy to operational environments or who perform clinical work for national security agencies must keep themselves informed regarding operational psychology roles, functions, and ethical dilemmas.

ROLES OF OPERATIONAL PSYCHOLOGISTS

In this section, we describe some of the most common operational psychology job functions and provide brief descriptions of the various roles and responsibilities these positions may entail.

Assessment and Selection

National security agencies (e.g., DoD, Directorate of National Intelligence, Central Intelligence Agency, National Security Agency) select personnel carefully (see chap. 2, this volume). In most of these agencies, the greatest danger that is posed is related to breaches of trust with highly classified information in positions of responsibility. In others, such as the DoD, the potential for harm ranges from individual shootings to the destruction of aircraft. These personnel may work in isolated environments with little sleep and in situations in which life and death decisions must be made routinely. The military began unprecedented assessment and screening procedures during World War I with the Army alpha and beta tests (Kennedy & McNeil, 2006; Yoakum & Yerkes, 1920), and in the 1940s the OSS (a precursor to the Central Intelligence Agency) pioneered specialized assessment and selection procedures for intelligence operatives (OSS, 1948).

The procedures used today have obviously evolved over time but remain a major focus for national security agencies. Unique processes exist for the assessment and selection of police officers (e.g., Arrigo & Claussen, 2003; Cochrane, Tett, & Vandecreek, 2003), special forces personnel (e.g., Banks, 2006; Bartone, Roland, Picano, & Williams, 2008; Milgram, 1991), intelligence personnel (OSS, 1948), aviators (e.g., Campbell, Moore, Poythress, & Kennedy, 2009; Carretta, 1992; Maschke, 2004), astronauts (e.g., Brady, 2005; Musson, Sandal, & Helmreich, 2004; Santy, 1994), and a variety of other high-risk and high-demand positions in national security agencies. Attributes that may be assessed for these positions include intellectual and cognitive abilities, emotional stability, initiative and motivation, character, physical fitness and a variety of other factors contributing to one's ability to maintain operational security (Picano et al., 2006). These evaluation procedures include a variety of psychological and neurocognitive tests, interviews, collateral history, physical examinations and tests, and background checks. Operational psychologists play key roles in the assessment and selection of personnel. Indeed, an early and narrower description of operational psychology was applied to preparing individuals for space travel, human factors, safety, and personnel selection in aviation and antiterrorism techniques (Williams et al., 2006).

Security Clearances

Evaluations of individuals for consideration or maintenance of a security clearance require specialized training. Although one must rule out any active mental health disorder and determine the prognosis for sobriety in the case of alcohol disorders, other issues must be carefully assessed (Bloom, 1993). For example, does the individual have any sexual practices that may jeopardize his or her ability to resist blackmail or other threats? Does the individual have personality characteristics that make him or her more likely to disclose protected information? Is the individual in an unhealthy relationship that jeopardizes his or her ability to make good decisions? Operational psychologists perform thorough evaluations to provide the most informed recommendations regarding someone's judgment and reliability for the safeguarding of classified information (see chap. 3, this volume).

Survival, Evasion, Resistance, and Escape Training

Operational psychologists play significant roles in the training provided at SERE schools. SERE psychologists train and educate those individuals who are at high risk of capture by an enemy. The SERE training includes surviving in austere environments, evading capture, resisting interrogation, and other techniques to maintain an advantage over one's captors and, when possible and appropriate, by escaping captors. Given the high-stress environment and the potential for both students and instructors to overidentify with their roles (e.g., begin to too closely identify themselves as prisoners or guards and start to maladaptively act and react accordingly; see Haney, Banks, & Zimbardo, 1973), psychologists are present for the majority of the training. Operational psychologists' primary roles include assessment and selection of SERE instructors, acting as a safety observer during high-risk phases of training (i.e., the capture and imprisonment scenario), educating both students and instructors, researching the effects of extreme stress on individuals, and assisting in the repatriation of U.S. prisoners of war (for a comprehensive review of SERE training, see Doran, Hoyt, & Morgan, 2006).

Repatriation of Personnel

In the role of repatriation, the operational SERE-trained psychologist initially assists the former U.S. detainee, prisoner of war, or hostage in the restoration of health and readjustment from the captivity situation by providing serial psychological assessment as needed as well as education regarding what to expect upon the individual's return and how to optimize his or her psychological adjustment (Doran et al., 2006). U.S. DoD (2000) directives and military service regulations note the well-being of the returnee to be the priority for the repatriated service member except in extreme circumstances (e.g., imminent danger to troops and a belief that the returnee may have information to prevent this). Given the high probability that repatriated personnel have information related to their captors (Stephenson & Staal, 2007) or other intelligence that may be critical to national security interests (Doran et al., 2006), the operational psychologist also assists in information-gathering sessions (i.e., debriefings). Operational psychologists generally moderate these intelligence debriefings to promote the psychological health of the returnee, allow for monitoring of any situation that may be detrimental to the mental health of the returnee, and to "advocate for protocols that maximize the accuracy of recalled information" (Doran et al., 2006, p. 255).

Counterintelligence and Counterterrorism

Counterintelligence and counterterrorism activities are among the newer roles performed by operational psychologists (see chap. 4, this volume). Support to counterintelligence operations may involve such activities as evaluating national security agency employees suspected of espionage, evaluating an intelligence operative to determine suitability to work under cover in enemy territory, or determining the suitability for recruitment of a potential intelligence resource (cf. OSS, 1948; Shumate & Borum, 2006). In doing so, the psychologist may provide both direct and indirect assessments (see the section on indirect assessments), consult to agency personnel, and support a number of agencies.

Consultation to Interrogation

Consultation to interrogation is perhaps the single component of the operational psychologist's role that is the least understood (see chap. 5, this volume; see also U.S. Department of Defense, 2009). Although the idea of military psychologists acting in this capacity is a newer development, police psychologists have been acutely aware of and involved in law enforcement's need to understand the dynamics of interrogation for some time (for a review, see Kassin & Gudjonsson, 2004). And while police psychologists are fully integrated into the law enforcement system, the individuals tasked with consulting to interrogations, the Behavioral Science Consultants (BSCs), continue their integration into the military's intelligence and detainee operation functions. Specifically, BSCs are defined as "psychologists and psychiatrists, not assigned to clinical practice functions, but to provide consultative services to support authorized law enforcement or intelligence activities, including detention and related intelligence, interrogation, and detainee debriefing operations" (U.S. Department of the Army, 2006, p. 4). Given the new role of psychologists serving as BSCs and the lessons learned from the earliest consultants (see James, 2008), the U.S. Army and the DoD produced a policy in 2006. Both clinical psychologists and operational psychologists have benefited. According to the DoD policy, "the mission of a BSC is to provide psychological expertise and consultation in order to assist the command in conducting safe, legal, ethical, and effective detention operations, intelligence interrogations, and detainee debriefing operations" (U.S. DoD, 2006, p. 5).

Further objectives of this policy are to ensure the humane treatment of detainees, prevent abuse, ensure the safety of U.S. personnel, and provide expertise to improve the effectiveness of interrogations and debriefing operations (Stephenson & Staal, 2007; U.S. Department of the Army, 2006; U.S. Department of Defense, 2009). Operational psychologists promote the rapport-building approach to interrogations as not only the most humane but also the most effective. Establishing a rapport develops a foundation in which questions are more likely to result in accurate and reliable information and assist in detecting deception (for a good illustration of an effective rapport-building approach to interrogation, see Alexander, 2008).

The policy also recognizes BSCs for their important role serving as advisors to interrogators:

> [The BSC acts] in a manner similar to psychologists assisting in criminal investigations, but does not plan, conduct or direct interrogations. The BSCT [Behavioral Science Consultation Team] also serves as yet another oversight mechanism; responsible for observing interrogators for "drift" in their personalities or interrogation practices that may tend toward unauthorized interrogation behavior. (U.S. Department of Defense, 2009, p. 62)

Indirect Assessments

Indirect assessments are typically performed when the individual (or group) in question cannot be directly examined and questions exist regarding personality, psychological functioning, intelligence, sociocultural issues, motivation, and/or behavior (see chap. 6, this volume). Within the realm of support to national security agencies provided by operational psychologists, this skill is applied in such areas as "criminal investigations, acts of terrorism, espionage, threat assessment, embezzlement, and disability fraud" (Morgan et al., 2006, p. 2). Information may come from a variety of sources that include behavioral checklists, multiple modes of surveillance, and even examination of an individual's trash. Historically, indirect assessments have been conducted on individuals as diverse as Adolf Hitler, Anwar al-Sadat, and Menachem Begin (see Williams et al., 2006).

The importance of understanding terrorism in general and terrorists in particular has been recognized for some time (see Beck, 2002; Holloway & Norwood, 1997; Zillmer, 2006). However, a primary focus of indirect assessment and profiling today obviously lies within this realm. Suicide terrorism has proven to be a complex issue that garners significant attention (Atran, 2003; Gordon, 2002; Pape, 2006). Other authors have analyzed the evolution of Al Qaeda (Sageman, 2004) and made predictions regarding future trends and jihadist goals that may lend assistance in effectively addressing the threat (Borum & Gelles, 2005). Moghaddam (2005) traced the decision-making process of individuals that eventually leads to terrorist acts and proposed a means to disrupt the process and prevent individuals from joining terrorist organizations. Sageman (2006) created a profile of Al Qaeda terrorists using open source material available from the Internet for 394 known terrorists. Understanding a threat makes it more likely that the threat can be effectively addressed, and operational psychologists are actively engaged in these activities.

Crisis and Hostage Negotiation

Psychologists' involvement in hostage negotiation largely grew out of the tragedy at the Munich Olympics in 1972, where terrorists took 11 hostages, all of whom were killed in the standoff, in addition to a police officer and 10 of the hostage takers. This spurred two police detectives from New York City (one of whom was a psychologist) to redefine the law enforcement response to hostage situations from one of a primary tactical mission to one of negotiation, a trend credited for a much higher rate of hostage survival (Rowe et al., 2006). Police psychologists, and to a lesser extent military psychologists, currently play key roles in these negotiations.

The roles of the operational psychologist in hostage negotiation consist of pre-, intra-, and postincident involvement. Prior to events, the operational psychologist participates in the screening and selection of negotiators and provides training on a wide variety of topics. Following negotiations, the psychologist provides stress management education and debriefings to personnel. However, it is during the incidents themselves that the unique skills of the operational psychologist come into play. During incidents, the operational psychologist monitors the negotiation and the stress level of the negotiator and provides consultation geared to optimize interactions with the hostage taker given his or her mental state. Indirect assessment strategies are used to understand the motivation of the hostage taker, optimizing the chances of bringing about a peaceful end to the situation. As with consulting to interrogations (see the section on consultation to interrogation), the operational psychologist has no direct contact with the hostage taker and acts solely as a consultant, providing valuable information and recommendations to the negotiation team (see chap. 6, this volume).

Conducting Psychological Autopsies

Psychological autopsies, or *equivocal death analyses*, are essentially indirect assessments conducted following an unexpected death to determine whether the death was the result of a homicide, suicide, or accidental causes. Psychologists review records and interview key individuals such as family members, coworkers, supervisors, friends, and roommates to ascertain circumstances and state of mind of the deceased at the time of the death (Gelles, 1995). By conducting an evaluation following the death, the psychologist surmises possible motives to commit suicide, current stressors potentially leading to a suicide at that particular time, and ways in which the individual typically managed stress. In this way, an understanding of the individual's personality is gleaned, and the events gain context. These findings assist medical examiners, forensic investigations, and policymakers.

PRINCIPAL ETHICAL DILEMMAS OF OPERATIONAL PSYCHOLOGISTS

With emerging roles for psychologists, new ethical questions have inevitably arisen. Guidance on some of these questions may be found easily in the 2002 APA "Ethical Principles of Psychologists and Code of Conduct" (Ethics Code; APA, 2010), whereas others require application of the Ethics Code in the context of military regulations and both U.S. and international law.

We should note that the development of ethical standards for new areas of psychological practice is a routine phenomenon. Psychologists in the American Association for Applied Psychology tackled the first Ethics Code in the 1930s (Coxe, 1939) even before the American Association for Applied Psychology and APA merged in the mid-1940s (Kennedy & McNeil, 2006). The work on the APA Ethics Code continued (APA, 1949; Hobbs, 1948) culminating in the *Ethical Standards of Psychologists* (APA, 1953). The Ethics Code has been revised nine times since its first version in direct response to changes in the practices and roles of psychologists. In some fields, standards have been developed that are uniquely applicable to those fields (e.g., research, forensics; APA, 1992; Perrin & Sales, 1994). The question has arisen as to whether the newer field of operational psychology requires changes to the 2010 Ethics Code or whether the Ethics Code is sufficient for use by these psychologists (e.g., APA, 2009). Discussion among the APA membership has centered around a discrepancy between the wording of the Introduction and Applicability section of the Ethical Principles of Psychologists and Code of Conduct and that of Ethical Standards 1.02 and 1.03, which address conflicts between ethics and law, and ethics and organizational demands. These standards are particularly relevant to operational psychologists. In response to requests that any discrepancy be addressed, in February 2010, the APA Council of Representatives voted that the language of both the Introduction and the Standards be amended, effective June 1, 2010 (APA, 2010). Amendments are in italics below:

From the Introduction and Applicability section:

If psychologists' ethical responsibilities conflict with law, regulations, or other governing legal authority, psychologists make known their commitment to this Ethics Code and take steps to resolve the conflict in a responsible manner in keeping with basic principles of human rights.

Ethical Standard 1.02:

1.02 Conflicts Between Ethics and Law, Regulations, or Other Governing Legal Authority
    If psychologists' ethical responsibilities conflict with law, regulations, or other governing legal authority, psychologists *clarify the nature of the conflict,* make known their commitment to the Ethics Code, and take *reasonable* steps to resolve the conflict *consistent with the General Principles and Ethical Standards of the Ethics Code. Under no circumstances may this standard be used to justify or defend violating human rights.*

Ethical Standard 1.03:

1.03 Conflicts Between Ethics and Organizational Demands
    If the demands of an organization with which psychologists are affiliated or for whom they are working are in conflict with this Ethics Code, psychologists clarify the nature of the conflict, make known their commitment to the Ethics Code, and *take reasonable steps to resolve the conflict consistent with the General Principles and Ethical Standards of the Ethics Code. Under no circumstances may this standard be used to justify or defend violating human rights.*

These changes emphasize the notion that apart from external obligations and constraints, important as they are, the internal motivation of psychologists to apply both the letter and spirit of the Ethics Code in their working lives is the foundation of professional ethics.

Although this categorization is certainly not all inclusive, the four principal dilemmas for operational psychologists may currently be classified as (a) mixed agency, (b) competence, (c) multiple relationships and (d) informed consent.

Mixed Agency

Defining the concept of mixed agency and providing ethical guidance related to divided loyalties have been struggles for the profession since the APA set forth its first Ethics Code (see Wiskoff, 1960). The APA's Task Force on the Role of Psychology in the Criminal Justice System, appointed in 1975, identified questions of loyalty as a leading concern (Monahan, 1980). A survey of police psychologists found this to be one of the top ethical concerns in police psychology (Zelig, 1988). Clinical military psychologists have grappled with the dilemma since they were first commissioned in World War II, and balancing the requirements of governmental agencies and the Ethics Code continues to be a routine challenge (Jeffrey, Rankin, & Jeffrey, 1992; Kennedy & Johnson, 2009). Having obligations to two or more entities simultaneously requires significant forethought and routine ethical analysis to manage.

The rapid evolution of the field of operational psychology has created newer and significantly complicated forms of mixed agency. For example, although BSCs have no clinical role and no direct contact with detainees about whom they may be consulting in an interrogation, the Ethics Code is clear that they have an obligation to that detainee (i.e., do no harm) as well as to the agency for which they work and to the general public (Behnke, 2006).

In the realm of operational psychology, the majority of the time the client is the military or other security agency, as opposed to the individual. Fortunately, there does exist a parallel for operational psychologists in the realm of forensic practice. Greenberg and Shuman (1997) noted some key variations between therapeutic and forensic roles, which are applicable for operational psychologists as well. Among these are having someone other than the individual deemed the client (i.e., the agency), differences in disclosure privilege (e.g., no traditional doctor–patient confidentiality), redefinition of competence (clinical evaluation vs. forensic evaluation), redefinition of the nature of the relationship (helping relationship vs. evaluative relationship), and redefinition of the goal of the relationship (therapeutic benefit vs. court benefit). In both cases there is no traditional doctor–patient relationship, and in both cases the psychologist may never meet the individual about whom he or she is consulting.

Dietz and Reese (1986) provided strategies for managing role conflicts when consulting to law enforcement agencies. Although 2 decades old, these strategies remain applicable to practice today. Perhaps most important are recommendations to provide the security agency with a copy of the APA Ethics Code, never compromise the individual being interviewed, make the agency fully aware of the extent of one's professional expertise, remain cognizant of the differences between the values and norms of psychologists and those of law enforcement, and maintain a stable identity to prevent overidentification with law enforcement.

The greatest area of divergence from traditional clinical practice, and perhaps the most difficult, is in cases in which the psychologist's input may have significant negative consequences for the individual. For example, in forensic psychology, an individual may be deemed capable of understanding right and wrong and participating in his or her own defense, opening him or her up for legal punishment for crimes. In the case of operational psychology, a psychologist may consult with negotiators to end a hostage situation only to have the negotiators decide that concerns for the safety of hostage(s) or for overall public safety are preeminent over the rights of the hostage taker, taking all necessary means to then resolve the hostage crisis (e.g., ordering a sniper to kill the hostage taker before he or she can harm a hostage). Mixed agency is difficult to navigate, and the operational psychologist must remain vigilant to effectively address it.

Competence

The issue of professional competence in an emerging field is also complicated largely because there are not yet established standards of practice (Staal & Stephenson, 2006), and this is identified as one of the primary ethical issues faced by the field of operational psychology (Johnson, 2002a; Williams et al., 2006). In addition to sound psychology practices, the operational psychologist must understand the agency and the mission of the agency for which he or she is working. To do this, Staal and Stephenson (2006) noted the need for operational psychologists to be trained in the Law of Armed Conflict, the Law of Land Warfare, the Geneva Conventions, and other applicable laws and regulations (e.g., U.S. Department of Army, 2006; U.S. DoD, 2006).

Because the field of operational psychology is evolving, established competencies have not yet been defined, as they have been in other areas of practice. This is not too surprising given that it has historically taken a significant amount of time to establish standards of competency in other fields. In the field of neuropsychology, for example, standards of competency have evolved over 2 decades, culminating in generally agreed upon education, training, and supervisory requirements (see APA Division 40, Clinical Neuropsychology, 1989, 2003; National Academy of Neuropsychology, 2001). Comparably, standards are emerging as they relate to competency in this new field of operational psychology. For example, the BSC policy clearly outlines prerequisites and training requirements for work in that operational area (U.S. Department of the Army, 2006) and Ritchie and Gelles (2002) set forth standards of training and quality assurance for the competent performance of psychological autopsies. As operational practice continues, standards of practice will continue to be defined and requirements for competency set. Toward this end, APA Division 18, Psychologists in Public Service, successfully advocated for the recognition of police psychology as a proficiency. To be deemed proficient one must exhibit competency in the areas of the "essential functions of police and public safety personnel, working conditions unique to their respective positions, common and novel stressors inherent in public safety work, normal and abnormal adaptation to occupational stress and trauma, research pertinent to resilience and recovery in public safety personnel, and the unique aspects of confidentiality and testimonial privilege when providing services to public safety personnel and/or agencies" (APA, 2008, para. 3).

Stephenson and Staal (2007) proposed that another way to address competency and operational psychology would be to make this a specialized area of practice requiring board certification.

In addition to technical competence, an operational psychologist must be capable of effectively contributing to national security efforts with a wide variety of populations from multiple countries and regions and with various religious and sociocultural backgrounds. In addition, operational psychologists must understand and be able to work within the law enforcement or military culture in which they are assigned. The military itself, for example, represents a unique cultural group with its own belief systems, language, and patterns of behavior (Reger, Etherage, Reger, & Gahm, 2008). Work with specialized groups such as special forces personnel requires an even greater level of cultural competence on the psychologist's part for operational consultation and selection activities to be effective.

Cultural competence in operational psychology cannot be overemphasized. It is worth noting that military clinical psychologists report significant and dramatic cultural variability in their patients, and most have been assigned either in combat zones of other countries and/or lived in a number of foreign countries (Kennedy, Jones, & Arita, 2007). Although these authors focused on military clinicians, they provided recommendations for both personal and professional development activities throughout the career to gain cultural competence in the highly diverse military environment, and these are applicable to operational psychologists as well.

Multiple Relationships

Multiple relationships, that is, having two or more roles with the same person, are another inherent challenge for psychologists serving government agencies and the military. Psychologists are often in positions in which there are few mental health resources and are subsequently tasked with activities that normally would be referred elsewhere (see Johnson, Ralph, & Johnson, 2005; Staal & King, 2000). In the military, for example, a clinical psychologist may be tasked with assessing a superior officer, a coworker, or even a roommate aboard ship (see Barnett & Yutrzenka, 2002; Zur & Gonzalez, 2002).

Operational psychologists, despite the fact that they are not performing primary clinical functions, are at risk of being placed in these situations. Remoteness of duty locations, the bond of shared danger, limited resources, and the preexisting established trust in the psychologist by coworkers present operational psychologists with the potential risk of entering into multiple relationships. Operational psychologists may be asked to perform a clinical assessment of a guard or police officer with psychological symptoms or to intervene face-to-face during an interrogation of a detainee if there is an emergency such as a suicidal statement.

Multiple relationships, however, are not all inherently unethical, which provides another challenge to operational psychologists. Given the frequency with which they arise, operational psychologists must be able to avoid potentially exploitative and/or harmful dual relationships but also recognize when such a relationship may be acceptable (see Lamb, Catanzaro, & Moorman, 2004; Younggren & Gottlieb, 2004).

Informed Consent

For some operational psychological activities, informed consent is standard. For example, in the case of evaluating an individual with alcohol dependence who is in remission for return of a security clearance, full written informed consent will be provided. The same is the case for traditional assessment and selection activities, such as those for high-risk occupational positions. However, the reality of operational psychology is that a number of duties are necessarily performed without informed consent and without confidentiality for the individual, with the rationale that to do so imperils the process and endangers the general public (cf. hostage negotiation, behavioral profiling of terrorists, etc.). For example, in the case of indirect assessments, there is no informed consent on the part of the individual or group of individuals being indirectly assessed. This involves a balancing act between weighing the rights of individuals who are suspected of a significant crime or plan to harm the interests of others and the welfare of society at large (Morgan et al., 2006).

CHALLENGES TO ETHICAL DECISION MAKING IN OPERATIONAL PSYCHOLOGY

Given the unique and highly variable nature of the demands placed on operational psychologists, there are challenges to their ability to engage in ethical decision making. The three challenges that could be considered most problematic are the lack of established standards of practice in the field, lack of available research literature, and the remoteness of work environments coupled with limited resources available for consultation.

Few Established Standards of Practice

Operational psychology is a relatively new field for which there exist few standards of practice. This creates opportunities for individuals to pioneer the field and to be in positions to make groundbreaking decisions. However, a reality of any newly evolving area of practice is that it is difficult to anticipate the types of ethical conflicts one may encounter (see, e.g., James, 2008). It also creates an increased risk of not realizing one has encountered an ethical conflict until after the fact. To address this important process of the ethical evolution of the field, individual operational psychologists have been pro-actively involving themselves in seeking out guidance from the APA and creating DoD instructions and regulations pertaining to psychologist support activities. These actions also have allowed operational psychologists to use these regulations to help educate their commanders, commanding officers, and other leaders about the nature of their activities and when their services may contribute to the mission and organizational requirements in an ethical and useful manner. Finally, operational psychologists are creating and participating in emerging training opportunities. Consistent with the recommendations found in Shumate and Borum (2006), there has been extensive collaboration between the military and other national security agencies in an effort to elucidate best practices by developing research questions and protocols, developing a relevant knowledge base, and recruiting top students to the field. In this way ethical dilemmas can be best addressed, and the field can be best developed.

Lack of Research Literature

The various fields of applied and clinical psychological practice further knowledge and provide information to students, peers, practitioners, the general public, and critics through dissemination of literature. The field of operational psychology, however, is not only in its infancy, but in the case of issues of national security, specific roles, actions, and even identities of psychologists may be deemed classified (Stephenson & Staal, 2007). This creates a situation in which operational psychologists may be unable to access a standard method of information delivery compared with other psychology specialties.

Because operational psychology is both a new field and one in which sensitive information may be at issue, manuscripts related to operational psychology and its support to missions may experience a delay for publication approval as military and government reviewers attempt to determine whether the information provided is classified or sensitive in nature. Although some aspects of the activities of operational psychology are classified, as this volume attests, much of what operational psychologists engage in is not. Accordingly, a DoD regulation regarding publications states that "clearance shall be granted if classified information is not disclosed, the DoD interests in nonclassified areas are not jeopardized, and the author accurately portrays official policy, even if the author takes issue with that policy" (U.S. DoD, 1996, p. 3). Fortunately, literature is slowly beginning to emerge, and through the efforts of operational psychologists, this risk is expected to diminish over time.

Isolated Work Environment

The secrecy and often isolated locations under which operational psychologists may find themselves working, along with the often compartmentalized nature of their work combine to make it difficult to consult with other psychologists as ethical issues arise. Staal and Stephenson (2006) noted a potential inability to consult with peers in these environments, cutting psychologists off from consultation resources and affecting their ability to engage in an ethical decision-making process. National security and security clearance issues also limit the breadth of resources these individuals may consult. To address the needs of military psychologists, the military psychology community has instituted a system of peer consultation, some of which is formalized (e.g., U.S. Navy psychology mentorship program). However, less experienced psychologists may need direct training on how to access, request, and use mentors, and individuals with the capability to mentor may also need training and guidance (Johnson, 2002b; Kaslow & Mascaro, 2007).

Despite challenges, there are multiple resources available to the operational psychologist. More reliable information technology resources significantly improve psychologists' ability to contact peers and mentors (e.g., through a classified Internet system for those with the requisite backgrounds and security clearances). As with any other psychology specialty, there are conferences and specialized continuing education opportunities (e.g., annual SERE conference, continuing education offerings from the DoD Counterintelligence Behavioral Science program), attendance at which should be a priority for operational psychologists. Much of the risk of the isolated work environment can be prevented by the operational psychologist by establishing support prior to assuming duties, enabling easy access to routine and emergent consultation when necessary.

OVERVIEW OF THIS BOOK

The volume begins with chapter 2 by Picano, Williams, Roland, and Long, in which they discuss assessment and selection procedures and ethical dilemmas encountered when assessing individuals for high-risk and high-demand jobs. In chapter 3, Young, Harvey, and Staal build on the assessment and selection chapter and discuss the challenges associated with evaluating individuals for high levels of security clearances. The roles of operational psychologists who consult to counterintelligence and counterterrorism agencies and the accompanying ethical dilemmas are discussed by Kennedy, Borum, and Fein in chapter 4. Dunivin, Banks, Staal, and Stephenson in chapter 5 describe the roles and ethical dilemmas faced by operational psychologists who consult to interrogations. Case examples that help to portray the roles of psychologists in these positions and give the reader a detailed look at the ethical decision-making process are provided. This is followed by Gelles and Palarea's analysis in chapter 6 of the issues encountered by operational psychologists who consult to crisis and hostage negotiations in a law enforcement environment. Finally, in chapter 7, we attempt to place the ethical issues in a broader context for this emerging field by establishing the evolving roles of operational psychology as linked to psychology's vital history and by addressing how with those emerging roles come new challenges to more clearly define and anchor an ethical practice of operational psychology.

CONCLUSION

The field of operational psychology, and subsequently its standards of practice, continue to be defined. The expansion of psychologists into new and evolving areas can be difficult. What follows in this volume are discussions of the predominant ethical issues currently being faced by operational psychologists in the context of their primary roles. Operational psychologists recognize the challenge and opportunity posed by this pioneering field, and with this volume, we seek to continue providing the ethical foundation on which to advance this area of practice.

REFERENCES

Alexander, M. (2008). *How to break a terrorist: The U.S. interrogators who used brains, not brutality, to take down the deadliest man in Iraq.* New York: Free Press.

American Psychological Association. (1949). Developing a code of ethics for psychologists. *American Psychologist, 4,* 17.

American Psychological Association. (1953). *Ethical standards of psychologists.* Washington, DC: Author.

American Psychological Association. (1992). *Ethical principles of psychologists and code of conduct.* Retrieved from http://www.apa.org/ethics/code/code-1992.aspx

American Psychological Association. (2008). *Public description of the proficiency of police psychology.* Retrieved from http://www.apa.org/ed/graduate/specialize/police.aspx

American Psychological Association. (2010). *Ethical principles of psychologists and code of conduct (2002, Amended June 1, 2010).* Retrieved from http://www.apa.org/ethics/code/index.aspx

American Psychological Association, Division 40, Clinical Neuropsychology. (1989). Definition of a clinical neuropsychologist. *The Clinical Neuropsychologist, 3,* 22.

American Psychological Association, Division 40, Clinical Neuropsychology. (2003). *Description of the specialty of clinical neuropsychology approved by APA Council of Representatives.* Retrieved May 19, 2008, from http://www.div40.org/def.html

American Psychological Association, Ethics Committee. (2009). *Call for language amending Ethical Standards 1.02 and 1.03.* Retrieved September 27, 2009, from http://www.apa.org/ethics/pdfs/language-2009.pdf

Arrigo, B. A., & Clauseen, N. (2003). Police corruption and psychological testing: A strategy for preemployment screening. *International Journal of Offender Therapy and Comparative Criminology, 47,* 272–290.

Atran, S. (2003, March). Genesis of suicide terrorism. *Science, 299,* 1534–1539.

Banks, L. M. (2006). The history of special operational psychological selection. In A. D. Mangelsdorff (Ed.), *Psychology in the service of national security* (pp. 83–95). Washington, DC: American Psychological Association.

Barnett, J. E., & Yutrzenka, B. A. (2002). Nonsexual dual relationships in professional practice, with special applications to rural and military communities. In A. A. Lazarus & O. Zur (Eds.), *Dual relationships and psychotherapy* (pp. 273–286). New York: Springer.

Bartone, P. T., Roland, R. R., Picano, J. J., & Williams, T. J. (2008). Psychological hardiness predicts success in US Army special forces candidates. *International Journal of Selection and Assessment, 16,* 78–81.

Beck, A. T. (2002). Prisoners of hate. *Behaviour Research and Therapy, 40,* 209–216.

Behnke, S. (2006, July–August). Ethics and interrogations: Comparing and contrasting the American Psychological, American Medical and American Psychiatric Association positions. *Monitor on Psychology, 37,* 66–67.

Bloom, R. W. (1993). Psychological assessment for security clearances, special access, and sensitive positions. *Military Medicine, 158,* 609–613.

Boring, E. G. (Ed.). (1945). *Psychology for the Armed Services.* Oxford, England: Infantry Journal.

Borum, R., & Gelles, M. (2005). Al-Qaeda's operational evolution: Behavioral and organizational perspectives. *Behavioral Sciences and the Law, 23,* 467–483.

Brady, J. V. (2005). Behavioral health: The propaedeutic requirement. *Aviation, Space, and Environmental Medicine, 76*, B13–B24.

Campbell, J. S., Moore, J. L., Poythress, N., & Kennedy, C. H. (2009). Personality traits in clinically referred aviators: Two clusters related to occupational suitability. *Aviation, Space, and Environmental Medicine, 80*, 1049–1054.

Carretta, T. R. (1992). Understanding the relations between selection factors and pilot training performance: Does the criterion make a difference? *The International Journal of Aviation Psychology, 2*, 95–105.

Cochrane, R. E., Tett, R. P., & Vandecreek, L. (2003). Psychological testing and the selection of police officers: A national survey. *Criminal Justice and Behavior, 30*, 511–537.

Coggins, M. H., Pynchon, M. R., & Dvoskin, J. A. (1998). Integrating research and practice in federal law enforcement: Secret service applications of behavioral science expertise to protect the President. *Behavioral Sciences and the Law, 16*, 51–70.

Coxe, W. W. (1939). Tentative report of the Committee on Professional Ethics, American Association for Applied Psychology, 1939. *Journal of Consulting Psychology, 4*, 24–26.

Dietz, P. E., & Reese, J. T. (1986). The perils of police psychology: 10 strategies for minimizing role conflicts when providing mental health services and consultation to law enforcement agencies. *Behavioral Sciences & the Law, 4*, 385–400.

Doran, A. P., Hoyt, G., & Morgan, C. A. (2006). Survival, evasion, resistance, and escape (SERE) training: Preparing military members for the demands of captivity. In C. H. Kennedy & E. A. Zillmer (Eds.), *Military psychology: Clinical and operational applications* (pp. 241–261). New York: Guilford Press.

Gelles, M. G. (1995). Psychological autopsy: An investigative aid. In M. I. Kurke & E. M. Scrivner (Eds.), *Police psychology into the 21st century* (pp. 337–355). Hillsdale, NJ: Erlbaum.

Gelles, M. G. (2007, April 5). Letter to Neil Altman, Uwe Jacobs, and Steven Miles. Retrieved March 15, 2008, from http://www.apa.org/ethics/pdfs/AltmanJacobs Milesresponseletter.pdf

Gordon, H. (2002). The "suicide" bomber: Is it a psychiatric phenomenon? *Psychiatric Bulletin, 26*, 285–287.

Greenberg, S. A., & Shuman, D. W. (1997). Irreconcilable conflict between therapeutic and forensic roles. *Professional Psychology: Research and Practice, 28*, 50–57.

Haney, C., Banks, C., & Zimbardo, P. (1973). Interpersonal dynamics in a simulated prison. *International Journal of Criminology & Penology, 1*, 69–97.

Hobbs, N. (1948). The development of a code of ethical standards for psychology. *American Psychologist, 3*, 80–84.

Holloway, H. C., & Norwood, A. E. (1997). Forensic psychiatric aspects of terrorism. In R. G. Lande & D. T. Armitage (Eds.), *Principles and practice of military forensic psychiatry* (pp. 409–451). Springfield, IL: Charles C Thomas.

James, L. C. (2008). Fixing hell: An Army psychologist confronts Abu Ghraib. New York: Grand Central.

Jeffrey, T. B., Rankin, R. J., & Jeffrey, L. K. (1992). In service of two masters: The ethical–legal dilemma faced by military psychologists. *Professional Psychology: Research and Practice, 23*, 91–95.

Johnson, W. B. (2002a). Consulting in the military context: Implications of the revised training principles. *Consulting Psychology Journal: Practice and Research, 54*, 233–241.

Johnson, W. B. (2002b). The intentional mentor: Strategies and guidelines for the practice of mentoring. *Professional Psychology: Research and Practice, 33*, 88–96.

Johnson, W. B., Ralph, J., & Johnson, S. J. (2005). Managing multiple roles in embedded environments: The case of aircraft carrier psychology. *Professional Psychology: Research and Practice, 36*, 73–81.

Kaslow, N. J., & Mascaro, N. A. (2007). Mentoring interns and postdoctoral residents in academic health sciences center. *Journal of Clinical Psychology in Medical Settings, 14*, 191–196.

Kassin, S. M., & Gudjonsson, G. H. (2004). The psychology of confessions: A review of the literature and issues. *Psychological Science in the Public Interest, 5*, 33–67.

Kennedy, C. H., & Johnson, W. B. (2009). Mixed agency in military psychology: Applying the American Psychological Association's ethics code. *Psychological Services, 6*, 22–31.

Kennedy, C. H., Jones, D. E., & Arita, A. A. (2007). Multicultural experiences of U.S. military psychologists: Current trends and training target areas. *Psychological Services, 4*, 158–167.

Kennedy, C. H., & McNeil, J. A. (2006). A history of military psychology. In C. H. Kennedy & E. A. Zillmer (Eds.), *Military psychology: Clinical and operational applications* (pp. 1–17). New York: Guilford Press.

Lamb, D. H., Catanzaro, S. J., & Moorman, A. S. (2004). A preliminary look at how psychologists identify, evaluate, and proceed when faced with possible multiple relationship dilemmas. *Professional Psychology: Research and Practice, 35*, 248–254.

Maschke, P. (2004). Personality evaluation of applicants in aviation. In K. Goeters (Ed.), *Aviation psychology: Practice and research* (pp. 141–151). Farnham, England: Ashgate.

McGuire, F. L. (1990). *Psychology aweigh: A history of clinical psychology in the United States Navy, 1900–1988.* Washington, DC: American Psychological Association.

Milgram, N. (1991). Personality factors in military psychology: In R. Gal & A. Mangelsdorff (Eds.), *Handbook of military psychology* (pp. 559–572). Chichester, England: Wiley.

Moghaddam, F. M. (2005). The staircase to terrorism: A psychological exploration. *American Psychologist, 60*, 161–169.

Monahan, J. (1980). *Who is the client? The ethics of psychological intervention in the criminal justice system.* Washington, DC: American Psychological Association.

Morgan, C. A., Gelles, M. G., Steffian, G., Coric, V., Temporini, H., Fortunati, F., et al. (2006). Consulting to government agencies: Indirect assessments. *Psychiatry, 3,* 2–6.

Musson, D. M., Sandal, G. M., & Helmreich, R. L. (2004). Personality characteristics and trait clusters in final stage astronaut selection. *Aviation, Space, and Environmental Medicine, 75,* 342–349.

National Academy of Neuropsychology. (2001). NAN definition of a clinical neuropsychologist.Retrieved March 29, 2008, from http://www.nanonline.org/NAN/Files/PAIC/PDFs/NANPositionDefNeuro.pdf

Office of Strategic Services. (1948). *Assessment of men: Selection of personnel for the Office of Strategic Services.* New York: Holt, Rinehart, & Winston.

Pape, R. A. (2006). Dying to win: The strategic logic of suicide terrorism. New York: Random House.

Perrin, G. I., & Sales, B. D. (1994). Forensic standards in the American Psychological Association's new ethics code. *Professional Psychology: Research and Practice, 25,* 376–381.

Picano, J. J., Williams, T. J., & Roland, R. R. (2006). Assessment and selection of high-risk operational personnel. In C. H. Kennedy & E. A. Zillmer (Eds.), *Military psychology: Clinical and operational applications* (pp. 353–370). New York: Guilford Press.

Reger, M. A., Etherage, J. R., Reger, G. M., & Gahm, G. A. (2008). Civilian psychologists in an Army culture: The ethical challenge of cultural competence *Military Psychology, 20,* 21–36.

Ritchie, E. C., & Gelles, M. G. (2002). Psychological autopsies: The current Department of Defense effort to standardize training and quality assurance. *Journal of Forensic Science, 47,* 1–3.

Rowe, K. L., Gelles, M. G., & Palarea, R. E. (2006). Crisis and hostage negotiation. In C. H. Kennedy & E. A. Zillmer (Eds.), *Military psychology: Clinical and operational applications* (pp. 310–330). New York: Guilford Press.

Sageman, M. (2004). *Understanding terror networks.* Philadelphia: University of Pennsylvania Press.

Sageman, M. (2006). The psychology of Al Qaeda terrorists: The evolution of the global Salafi jihad. In C. H. Kennedy & E. A. Zillmer (Eds.), *Military psychology: Clinical and operational applications* (pp. 281–294). New York: Guilford Press.

Santy, P. (1994). Choosing the right stuff: The psychological selection of astronauts and cosmonauts. New York: Praeger.

Shumate, S., & Borum, R. (2006). Psychological support to defense counterintelligence operations. *Military Psychology, 18,* 283–296.

Staal, M. A., & King, R. E. (2000). Managing a multiple relationship environment: The ethics of military psychology. *Professional Psychology: Research and Practice, 31,* 698–705.

Staal, M. A., & Stephenson, J. A. (2006). Operational psychology: An emerging sub-discipline. *Military Psychology, 18*, 269–282.

Stephenson, J. A., & Staal, M. A. (2007). Operational psychology: What constitutes expertise? *The Specialist, 26,* 13, 30–31.

Summers, F. (2007). Psychoanalysis, the American Psychological Association, and the involvement of psychologists at Guantanamo Bay. *Psychoanalysis, Culture & Society, 12,* 83–92.

U.S. Department of the Army. (2006). *OTSG/MEDCOM Policy Memo 06-029: Behavioral science consultation policy.* Fort Sam Houston, TX: Author.

U.S. Department of Defense. (1996). *Department of Defense Instruction 5230.9: Clearance of DoD information for public release.* Washington, DC: Author.

U.S. Department of Defense. (2000). *Department of Defense Instruction 2310.4: Repatriation of prisoners of war (POW), hostages, peacetime government detainees and other missing or isolated personnel.* Washington, DC: Author.

U.S. Department of Defense. (2006). *Department of Defense Instruction 2310.8E: Medical program support for detainee operations.* Washington, DC: Author.

U.S. Department of Defense (2009). *Review of department compliance with President's executive order on detainee conditions of confinement.* Washington, DC: Author. Retrieved May 22, 2009, from http://www.defenselink.mil/pubs/pdfs/REVIEW_OF_DEPARTMENT_COMPLIANCE_WITH_PRESIDENTS_EXECUTIVE_ORDER_ON_DETAINEE_CONDITIONS_OF_CONFINEMENTa.pdf

Wells, G. L., Malpass, R. S., Lindsay, R. C. L., Fisher, R. P., Turtle, J. W., & Fulero, S. M. (2000). From the lab to the police station: A successful application of eye witness research. *American Psychologist, 55,* 581–198.

Williams, T. J., & Johnson, W. B. (2006). Introduction to the special issue: Operational psychology and clinical practice in operational environments. *Military Psychology, 18,* 261–168.

Williams, T. J., Picano, J. J., Roland, R. R., & Banks, L. M. (2006). Introduction to operational psychology. In C. H. Kennedy & E. A. Zillmer (Eds.), *Military psychology: Clinical and operational applications* (pp. 193–214). New York: Guilford Press.

Wiskoff, M. (1960). Ethical standards and divided loyalties. *American Psychologist, 15,* 656–660.

Yerkes, R. M. (1918). Psychology in relation to war. *Psychological Review, 25,* 85–115.

Yerkes, R. M. (1919). Report of the psychology committee of the National Research Council. *Psychological Review, 26,* 83–149.

Yoakum, C. S., & Yerkes, R. M. (1920). *Army mental tests.* New York: Holt.

Younggren, J. N., & Gottlieb, M. C. (2004). Managing risk When contemplating multiple relationships. *Professional Psychology: Research and Practice, 35,* 255–260.

Zeidner, J., & Drucker, A. J. (1988). *Behavioral science in the Army: A corporate history of the Army Research Institute.* Washington, DC: Army Research Institute.

Zelig, M. (1988). Ethical dilemmas in police psychology. *Professional Psychology: Research and Practice*, *19*, 336–338.

Zillmer, E. A. (2006). The psychology of terrorists: Nazi perpetrators, the Baader-Meinhof gang, war criminals in Bosnia, and suicide bombers. In C. H. Kennedy & E. A. Zillmer (Eds.), *Military psychology: Clinical and operational applications* (pp. 262–280). New York: Guilford Press.

Zur, O., & Gonzalez, S. (2002). Multiple relationships in military psychology. In A. A. Lazarus & O. Zur (Eds.), *Dual relationships and psychotherapy* (pp. 315–328). New York: Springer.

2

OPERATIONAL PSYCHOLOGISTS IN SUPPORT OF ASSESSMENT AND SELECTION: ETHICAL CONSIDERATIONS

JAMES PICANO, THOMAS J. WILLIAMS, ROBERT ROLAND, AND CARLA LONG

Operational psychologists are often involved in developing and staffing assessment and selection programs for personnel involved in high-risk operational missions (Picano, Williams, & Roland, 2006). Operational psychology support for assessment and selection programs may include the design and development of assessment and selection processes and procedures as well as research and validation studies of assessment and selection methods and decisions based on real-world operational outcomes (Williams, Picano, Roland, & Banks, 2006).

Picano et al. (2006) defined *high-risk operational personnel* as those who undertake missions that involve nonstandard or unconventional occupational demands, often in politically sensitive, hostile, or extreme operating environments and often in various cultural settings. Such missions present many unknown and often uncontrollable factors in which an individual's success depends on his or her ingenuity, expertise, initiative, and a high degree of common sense to avoid mission failure (Picano et al., 2006). Although our

The views expressed in this article are those of the authors and do not reflect the official policy or position of the U.S. Department of the Army, U.S. Department of Defense, or the U.S. Government.

29

experience is mostly with military operational personnel, there are other occupations that clearly fit within this definition (e.g., astronauts, bomb disposal personnel; for a review, see Flin, 2001).

Psychologists who provide assessment and selection services in operational settings must confront a number of ethical issues. Such issues arise from the unique contexts and settings in which operational psychologists work, the differing needs of agencies and organizations, as well as the multiple roles that psychologists may play in operational settings. Most often operational psychologists engaged in the assessment and selection of high-risk operational personnel work in military or other government agencies. Such settings present their own unique ethical challenges (Ewing & Gelles, 2003; Johnson, 1995, 2002). Nevertheless, the ethical issues confronting operational psychologists who engage in assessment and selection of individuals for high-risk operational missions are not unlike those confronted by other psychologists who are involved in applications of assessment outside of traditional psychology settings for other high-reliability personnel such as police psychologists. In more traditional settings, somewhat similar ethical issues are often faced by school psychologists (Lumsden, Bore, Millar, Jack, & Powis, 2005) and forensic psychologists (Bush, Connell, & Denney, 2006).

Our goal in this chapter is to highlight some of the ethical challenges facing operational psychologists who engage in the assessment and selection of high-risk operational personnel. Given the potential impact on the lives and livelihood of those for whom selection procedures are used, the foundation for ethical practice in this area is Principle A, Beneficence and Nonmaleficence, of the American Psychological Association's (APA's) "Ethical Principles of Psychologists and Code of Conduct" (Ethics Code), which states: "Because psychologists' scientific and professional judgments and actions may affect the lives of others, they are alert to and guard against personal, financial, social, organizational, or political factors that might lead to misuse of their influence" (APA, 2010).

In this chapter, we specifically address ethical issues in the areas of competency, such as the qualifications and experience required to engage in the assessment and selection of high-risk operational personnel, informed consent, and limits of confidentiality and privacy. We also discuss professional responsibilities and provide some guidelines for the ethical practice of assessment and selection for high-risk operational personnel. However, we first begin by introducing and briefly reviewing some of the legal issues of relevance to any psychologist involved in personnel selection. A detailed discussion of the legal challenges in personnel selection is beyond the scope of this chapter (see, e.g., Sampson & Lyons, 1990).

LEGAL ISSUES IN THE ASSESSMENT AND SELECTION OF HIGH-RISK OPERATIONAL PERSONNEL

Congress and the courts have generally exempted the uniformed services from coverage by broad cross-cutting federal employment legislation (such as the Americans With Disabilities Act [ADA] of 1990), preferring that equal employment opportunities in the uniformed services be enforced through specific policies implemented by the U.S. Department of Defense through the chain of command. However, federal legislation could apply and most often does to civilian personnel when they seek employment within the U.S. Department of Defense and certainly applies to those seeking employment within other government agencies. Thus, operational psychologists conducting assessment and selection must be familiar with landmark legislation in this area.

The legal landscape in which personnel selection is practiced has been altered dramatically over the past 2 decades as a result of important legislative acts as well as developments in case law. The overall intent of such legislation is to prohibit unfair discrimination in employment and provide equal employment opportunity for all. The U.S. Equal Employment Opportunity Commission (EEOC; Uniform Guidelines on Employee Selection Procedures, 1978) is the federal agency charged with enforcing laws relevant to personnel selection and ensuring that all employment evaluation procedures are administered fairly and consistently to all applicants. Employment laws apply to all private employers and federal, state, and local governments. Within federal agencies more specifically, the Civil Service Reform Act (CSRA) of 1978 was designed to promote fairness in personnel actions and prohibits discrimination against applicants for employment on the basis of race, color, national origin, religion, sex, age, or disability. Of note, the CSRA does not apply to the Federal Bureau of Investigation or any executive agency whose principal function concerns the conduct of foreign intelligence or counterintelligence activities.

Psychologists engaged in the assessment and selection of high-risk operational personnel must be familiar with the federal laws relevant to this area of practice. Two of the more important recent legislative acts include the ADA, and the Civil Rights Act of 1991.

The ADA prohibits employment discrimination against qualified individuals with disabilities and applies to employment opportunities in the private sector as well as in state and local governments (Enforcement Guidance: Preemployment Disability-Related Questions and Medical Examinations, 1995). Specifically, the ADA forbids inquiries regarding the existence, nature, or severity of a disability before an individual has been given an offer of employment, even if such inquiries are job related (Tippins, 2002). Once an applicant has been given a conditional job offer, an employer may make disability-related inquiries and conduct medical evaluations (including psychological evaluations) regardless of whether they are job related, provided they are required of all applicants:

> An employer may require an applicant or employee to undergo a medical examination, *i.e.*, a procedure or test that seeks information about an individual's physical or mental impairments or health. The ADA also specifies when an employer may make "disability-related inquiries," *i.e.*, inquiries that are likely to elicit information about a disability. When hiring, an employer may not ask questions about disability or require medical examinations until *after* it makes a conditional job offer to the applicant. After making a job offer (but before the person starts working), an employer may ask disability-related questions and conduct medical examinations as long as it does so *for all individuals entering the same job category*. 42 U.S.C. §12112 (d)(2) & (3). [emphasis added]

From a practical perspective, the ADA has significantly altered the practice of selection testing because clearly most psychological and personality tests used for screening are considered *medical tests*. If the psychological testing is being done to screen for or diagnose a mental illness, then both the ADA and the EEOC restrict these activities. However, if the psychological or personality testing is being completed to identify personality traits such as honesty, preferences, or habits, it may not qualify as a medical test (see, e.g., *Karraker v. Rent-A-Center, Inc.*, 2005). Therefore, caution is advised when considering psychological testing in support of assessment and selection activities. The following factors provide guidance to help determine whether a psychological test is considered a medical test:

- Is the test being administered by a psychologist or other health care provider?
- Is the test designed to assess and/or reveal the presence of an impairment or to establish the mental or physical health status of an individual?
- Does the test measure physiological (e.g., polygraph) or psychological responses as opposed to a specific task that an individual must perform (e.g., job center)?
- Does the test tend to screen out any individuals or class of individuals with disabilities unless the test has been shown to select for job-related attributes consistent with business necessity?
- Does the test accurately reflect the skills, aptitude, and other attributes that it purports to assess while ensuring that it does not reflect the applicant's impairment?
- Does the test allow for a reasonable accommodation for any known physical and/or mental limitations considered relevant

for the job without creating an undue hardship on employer, the testing conditions, or the prospective employee?

It is important to note that the EEOC has determined that psychological tests designed to identify a mental disorder or impairment (such as the Minnesota Multiphasic Personality Inventory—2; Butcher, Dahlstrom, Graham, Tellegen, & Kaemmer, 1989) are considered medical examinations and thus may not be used prior to a conditional offer of employment. It is important that psychological tests used to measure personality traits that are important determinants of work behaviors and productivity (cf. Guion & Gottier, 1965) as well as tests to determine integrity and drug use (see, e.g., Sackett, Burris, & Callahan, 1989) are not considered medical examinations (Uniform Guidelines on Employee Selection Procedures, 1978) and may be used preoffer if job relevant.

We have compiled a summary of federal agency guidance documents pertaining to the ADA. These are presented in Exhibit 2.1.

Another important piece of legislation is the Civil Rights Act of 1991. Among other things, the Civil Rights Act of 1991 provides for monetary

EXHIBIT 2.1

Federal Agency Guidance Documents for the Americans With Disabilities Act

Interpretive Guidance Accompanying the Title I Regulations (also known as the "Appendix" to the Regulations), 29 C.F.R. pt. 1630 app. §§ 1630.2(o), (p), 1630.9.
   Enforcement Guidance on Reasonable Accommodation and Undue Hardship Under the Americans With Disabilities Act. 8 FEP Manual 405:7601(1999).

1. Enforcement Guidance: Preemployment Disability-Related,Questions and Medical Examinations at 5, 6-8, 20, 21-22. 8 FEP Manual (BNA) 405:7191, 7192-94. 7201 (1995).
2. Enforcement Guidance: Workers' Compensation and the ADA at 1520, 8 FEP Manual (BNA) 405:7391, 7398–7401 (1996).
3. Enforcement Guidance: the Americans with Disabilities Act and Psychiatric Disabilities at 19-28, 8 FEP Manual (BNA) 405.7461, 7470-76 (1997).
4. Fact Sheet on the Family and Medical Leave Act, the Americans With Disabilities Act, and Title VII of the Civil Rights Act of 1964 at 6-99 8 FEP Manual (BNA) 405-7371, 7374-76 (1996).
5. Enforcement Guidance: Disability-Related Inquiries and Medical Examinations of Employees Under the Americans With Disabilities Act at 20, 22, 23, 24.

   A Technical Assistance Manual on the Employment Provisions (Title I) of the Americans With Disabilities Act, 8 FEP Manual (BNA) 405:6981, 6998-7018 (1992) (Technical Assistance Manual, which includes a 200-page Resource Directory, including federal and state agencies and disability organizations that can provide assistance in identifying and locating reasonable accommodations).
   Information retrieved June 29, 2008, from http://www.eeoc.gov/policy/docs/factemployment_procedures.html

damages in cases of intentional employment discrimination. Relevant to the practice of personnel selection, this act also defined separate race norming for selection measures as discriminatory, and hence illegal.

Before we end our discussion of the legal issues involved in assessment and selection of high-risk operational personnel, one illustrative case, *Soroka v. Dayton Hudson Corporation* (1991), deserves brief discussion. *Soroka* was a California case that challenged the Dayton Hudson Corporation's practice of requiring applicants for security officers at its Target stores to take psychological tests as part of their preemployment screening. The issues of the case dealt with an individual's right to privacy with respect to intrusiveness of test items, especially those that inquired about sexual orientation, religious beliefs, and political views. The plaintiffs argued that use of psychological tests with intrusive items invaded their privacy. They also alleged discrimination on the basis of religion and sexual orientation. The trial court found that the use of psychological tests for screening security officers was reasonable and that Target had a legitimate business interest in screening emotional stability in their security officer applicants. However, the California Court of Appeals later reversed the trial court decision, finding that the potential harm caused to applicants by the continuing use of the psychological tests outweighed the harm caused to Target by prohibiting their use. Although the case was slated for review by the California Supreme Court, an out-of-court settlement between the parties was reached before that review.

Camera and Merenda (2000) provided a thoughtful and thorough review of the factual evidence in *Soroka* and the case's implications for the use of personality tests in preemployment screening. These authors warned that psychologists who use clinical instruments in making decisions in employment settings may be on "thin ice," as many are illegal under the ADA, and others lack evidence of validity for their use with job applicants. No doubt in large part as a result of legislation such as the ADA and cases like *Soroka*, test publishers have looked carefully at their products. Some have developed revised versions of highly used personality inventories (e.g., 16 Personality Factors [Cattell, Cattell, & Cattell, 1993] and the NEO-4 [Costa & McCrae, 1998]) that are compliant with the ADA by omitting items that unnecessarily intrude into individuals' privacy.

Given that the job tasks of security officers were at issue in *Soroka* and that these were clearly differentiated from those of a police officer in both scope and complexity, the findings have been interpreted as not applying to police officers and other high-risk personnel (Flanagan, 1995). However, because the California Supreme Court never ruled on the case, this is still unresolved. Thus, operational psychologists who use clinical measures to assess emotional stability should ensure that the measures used are appropriate for the purpose of the evaluation. In particular, operational psychologists should be extremely cautious about using measures of psychopathology or impairment for employment screening in the preoffer stage.

In summary, the laws pertaining to the assessment of high-risk operational personnel are complex and may or may not be applicable to every setting. Many operational psychologists practice in government agencies that sponsor selection programs for high-risk operational personnel and must comply with departmental or agency regulations and directives governing their selection efforts. Fortunately, operational psychologists practicing in these settings often have access to staff legal counsel. Thus, we recommend that whenever possible operational psychologists consult with the appropriate legal authority to ensure that their processes and procedures comply with the applicable federal laws and/or departmental regulations.

ETHICAL STANDARDS AND ASSESSING HIGH-RISK OPERATIONAL PERSONNEL

As Staal and Stephenson (2006) noted, military psychology has long struggled with significant ethical issues, predominant among them concerns about confidentiality, multiple roles, and requests for services by third parties (see Exhibit 2.2 for the content of these standards).

EXHIBIT 2.2
Ethical Standards of Primary Interest to Military Psychologists

Ethical Standard 4.01, Maintaining Confidentiality
Psychologists have a primary obligation and take reasonable precautions to protect confidential information obtained through or stored in any medium, recognizing that the extent or limits of confidentiality may be regulated by law, or established by institutional rules, or professional or scientific relationships.

Ethical Standard 3.05, Multiple Relationships
A psychologist refrains from entering into a multiple relationship if the multiple relationship could reasonably be expected to impair the psychologist's objectivity, competence, or effectiveness in performing his or her functions as a psychologist, or otherwise risks exploitation or harm to the person with whom the professional relationship exists.

Ethical Standard 3.07, Third-Party Requests for Services
(a) When psychologists agree to provide services to a person or entity at the request of a third party, psychologists clarify at the outset of the service, the nature of the relationship with all individuals or organizations involved. This clarification includes the role of the psychologist . . . , the probable uses of the services provided or the information obtained, and the fact there may be limits to confidentiality.

From "Ethical Principles of Psychologists and Code of Conduct," by the American Psychological Association, 2010. Available at http://www.apa.org/ethics/code/index.aspx. Copyright 2010 by the American Psychological Association.

Recognition of this struggle prompted the APA Ethics Committee (1993) to issue a special policy statement that recommended taking preventive, proactive steps to discuss potential problem areas with supervisors and to remain vigilant for appropriate alternatives to the practical dilemmas that are certain to arise.

Johnson (2002) discussed these issues in the context of the unique dynamics that differentiate the military from other organizations. He highlighted the mission orientation of the military, which is primarily to defend the country, as well as the imperative of military psychologists to place military interests first (such as the lawful orders of the officers appointed over them in support of mission achievement), sometimes in direct conflict with their own (e.g., professional ethics and personal safety within a war zone) and others' needs. Despite these ethical challenges, the routine duties of military psychologists working in clinical settings do not diverge dramatically from those of their nonmilitary peers (Williams & Johnson, 2006).

The situation is quite different for operational psychologists. These individuals often apply their psychological training and skills in direct support of combat operations, intelligence missions, and other national security operations (Williams & Johnson, 2006; Williams et al., 2006). In military settings, operational psychology involves military psychologists working outside of their traditional clinical roles to assist commanders in executing combat operations (Staal & Stephenson, 2006). To further differentiate the role of operational psychologists from those of traditional military psychologists who might be plying their craft in a combat zone, Staal and Stephenson (2006) considered the work of an operational psychologist as one more in support of an intelligence function (as opposed to the more traditional and accepted medical function) with end products contributing to the commander's operational decision making. In this conceptualization, the operational psychologist may operate as a member of the commander's special (as opposed to medical) staff and thereby be subject to designation as a military combatant under the rules of the Geneva Convention. However, similar to other psychologists operating outside more traditional clinical roles, operational psychologists still have an ethical obligation to abide by the Ethics Code within the context of the psychological services they provide.

Assessment and selection of personnel for special duty or high-risk operational assignments is a core function associated with operational psychologists (Picano et al., 2006; Staal & Stephenson, 2006; Williams et al., 2006). In this work, operational psychologists draw on the core competencies and training in assessment common to all psychologists. However, the often high stakes and unique organizational contexts and applications of operational assessment and selection bring with them additional ethical and professional responsibilities. Consequently, we recommend that operational psychologists who engage in assessment and selection of high-risk operational personnel become thoroughly familiar with the Ethics Code (APA, 2010) and the *Standards for Educational and Psychological Testing* (APA, 1999).

Competence

Standard 2.01, Boundaries of Competence, of the Ethics Code (APA, 2010) requires that psychologists provide services "with populations and in areas only within the boundaries of their competence based on education, training, supervised experience, consultation, study, or professional experience" (p.1063). With respect to assessment, psychologists are expected to demonstrate the many competencies needed for minimally competent use and choice of tests, use of instructions, application of procedures, and interpretations (Moreland, Eyde, Robertson, Primoff, & Most, 1995).

> Relatedly, although psychological tests can assist clinicians with case formulation and treatment recommendations, they are only tools. Tests do not think for themselves, nor do they directly communicate with patients. Like a stethoscope, a blood pressure gauge, or an MRI scan, a psychological test is a dumb tool, and the worth of the tool cannot be separated from the sophistication of the clinician who draws inferences from it. (Meyer et al., 2001, p. 153)

Similar to other emerging specialty areas, defining the boundaries of competent practice as an operational psychologist, generally, and in the assessment and selection of high-risk operational personnel, specifically, is difficult. As is true of many of the functions of operational psychologists, the psychological assessment and selection of high-risk operational personnel draws on knowledge and skills that cut across diverse specialties of psychology. In her discussion of the uses of individual assessment for personality selection, Kwaske (2004) observed that training in personnel selection within the different specialties of psychology is probably insufficient for competent practice, though the inadequacies associated with each of the specialties are different. She noted, for example, that clinical and counseling psychologists receive the bulk of their training in using clinical skills such as behavioral observation, interviewing, and testing; whereas industrial and organizational psychologists receive the bulk of their training and education in aspects of personnel psychology including job analysis, measurement, and legal issues.

It appears that professional psychology training models for complex activities involved in the assessment of high-risk operational personnel have always been insufficient. During World War II, psychologists participating in the assessment and selection of personnel for clandestine operations for the Office of Strategic Services (OSS), the forerunner of modern day operational assessment and selection programs, noted limitations in the prevailing training model of the day for preparing clinical psychologists for work in operational assessment and selection. They recognized that psychologists required more training in the "use of concepts, testing procedures, and statistics appropriate to exploration of normal personalities" (Fiske, Hanfmann, MacKinnon, Miller, & Murray, 1948/1997, p. 473). These prominent psychologists recommended 6- to 12-month training experiences in university-based assessment centers devoted to understanding personality. A few of these institutes were set up across the country at prominent universities (e.g., the Institute for Personality Assessment and Research at the University of California, Berkeley), and their contributions to psychologists' understanding and assessment of normal personality have been monumental.

We have previously detailed the need for contemporary operational psychologists to develop competencies in the complexities involved in multicultural assessments (Williams et al., 2006) and especially in the psychometric issues complicating multicultural assessment. Staal and Stephenson (2006) also highlighted these complexities in their description of a recent assessment and selection effort designed to select Iraqi soldiers for an elite special forces unit. Given that the world has entered what many national security experts describe as an era of persistent conflict, it is reasonable to expect that operational psychologists involved in the assessment and selection of high-risk operational personnel will continue to find themselves challenged by the need to assess individuals from varying cultures, both within the United States as well as multinationally. Thus, the development of competencies in multicultural assessment would appear to be a pressing need. Development of needed competencies can often be met through continuing education and training courses in multicultural assessment. However, many of the cultures within which operational psychologists may find themselves are cultures in which basic freedoms and human rights have been denied. Consequently, the accepted academic approaches (e.g., surveying members of a population, ethnographic studies) to gain a better understanding of individuals within a culture oftentimes do not exist. Indeed, as is the generally accepted case within academia, those individuals who have lived and/or operated within these denied areas may serve as the most authoritative source of information for operational psychologists. In view of the extant risk and danger, operational psychologists may often serve as the authoritative source with the most experience in denied areas. Given the breadth of potential experiences and opportunities, it is vital that operational psychologists seek consultation from subject matter experts in multicultural assessment.

Operational psychologists must take care to ensure they possess or develop all of the complex skill sets necessary for competent practice in the assessment and selection of high-risk operational personnel. In some cases, the complexity involves the ability to understand and extrapolate the unique mission and requisite support requirements. Operational psychologists must be alert to the possibility of practicing outside their areas of competence and should seek the services of other psychologists or professionals when assessment projects require expertise outside their competencies. For example, Lowman (1998) described a case of ethical practice in which an industrial and organizational psychologist consulted with a clinical psychologist to assess the emotional stability of candidates in personnel selection. Assessment and selection programs for high-risk operational personnel within the U.S. Department of Defense, where we have the bulk of our experience, whether by design or by necessity, often comprise teams of psychologists with complementary skills and representing several (e.g., clinical, industrial and organizational, social) specialties. We believe this to be the ideal of competent practice in complex operational assessment and selection programs.

Unfortunately, the sensitive nature of operational selection programs and the security requirements for entry into these programs limit access to psychologists without appropriate security clearances for consultation and training purposes. For those with the appropriate security clearances, access can be provided on a *need-to-know* basis and is often limited in scope. Security considerations also often preclude publication of the processes and methods used by operational selection psychologists, further limiting the opportunities for external peer review and process improvement. Nonetheless, the security considerations are more analogous to proprietary concerns that commercial entities may express than to an effort to keep others from monitoring and/or evaluating the process. Perhaps some reassurance is possible in light of the consideration that assessment and selection procedures do not differ significantly from those developed for the OSS by several esteemed psychologists.

Operational psychologists also attend professional conferences and meetings sponsored by government agencies that provide a forum in which they can present their work to others engaged in similar activities to obtain needed consultation and peer review to ensure the competence of their work. In addition, within the U.S. Department of Defense, there is command oversight of specialized operational assessment and selection programs that includes periodic inspection of the psychological practices in the program by outside experienced operational psychologists. This helps to ensure that operational selection processes are valid and reflect responsible standards of practice.

Confidentiality

Ethical Standard 4.01, Maintaining Confidentiality, specifically addresses the limits of confidentiality and requires psychologists to disclose to individuals at the outset of the relationship both the limits of confidentiality and the foreseeable uses of information generated through psychological activities. Within operational settings, departmental or agency directives mandate disclosure of confidential material to those with a need to know, such as a military commander or other operational decision maker. Thus, in operational assessment and selection programs there is no guarantee of confidentiality for those applicants who volunteer to participate. Nothing revealed to the psychologist orally, in writing, or in response to psychological test questions can be considered confidential. Evaluation results are released in reports to agency personnel as part of the evaluation of an individual's overall suitability for high-risk positions. This puts psychologists in direct conflict with their ethical obligations to those who are evaluated (London & Bray, 1980). Under such conditions, operational psychologists are ethically obligated to inform individuals of the absence of confidentiality.

In practice, operational psychologists involved in the assessment and selection of high-risk operational personnel have managed to negotiate this process fairly easily through the use of written informed consents and by taking great effort to respect individuals' privacy. Experienced operational psychologists generally release only relevant information to satisfy program requirements without divulging unnecessary information that does not bear on a selection decision. In short, operational psychologists "disclose the minimum amount of information that is necessary to achieve the purpose" (APA, 2010). In the operational environments in which we have worked, surprisingly few decision makers have been interested in any of the details that informed the psychologist's recommendation, and all of the program managers with whom we have worked respected the individual's right to privacy. We believe this reflects the benefit of and reinforces the importance of operational psychologists helping to educate leaders and decision makers about ways to reduce the potential conflict between professional ethics and organizational practices.

But what about other disclosures? The 2002 Ethics Code substantially relaxes the prohibitions against disclosure of information to individuals and third parties and grants psychologists greater discretion in releasing information in part so that psychologists are better able to comply with the requirements for release of information under the Health Insurance Portability and Accountability Act (HIPAA). It is not clear whether individuals can request some or all of the test results and interview notes gathered as part of an assessment and selection program under HIPAA. This may be determined by whether such information is considered part of a medical record (see also Spychalski, 2003) in conjunction with the psychologist's status (e.g., health care professional) as well as whether the agency is considered a covered entity under HIPAA.

In addition, many assessment and selection programs for high-risk operational personnel are situated in federal agencies or in the U.S. Department of Defense. As Spychalski (2003) noted, the Freedom of Information Act of 1996 (FOIA) allows for records in the possession of agencies or departments of the U.S. government to be accessible to the public. However, to the extent that psychological assessment and selection data reflect private, personal information as well as information related to deliberative and predecisional actions, they are specifically exempted from release under the FOIA, as such disclosure would compromise the objectivity or fairness of the assessment process (Spychalski, 2003).

Informed Consent

It is not completely clear whether operational psychologists are ethically obligated to obtain informed consent from applicants in assessment and selection programs for high-risk operational jobs. According to the Ethics Code (Standard 3.10a), psychologists must obtain informed consent when providing research, assessment, therapy, counseling, or consultation services "except when conducting such activities without consent is mandated by law or governmental regulation or as otherwise provided in this Ethics Code" (APA, 2010). Elsewhere the Ethics Code (Standard 9.03a) states that psychologists obtain informed consent for assessments *except* when "informed consent is implied because testing is conducted as a routine educational, institutional, or organizational activity (e.g., when participants voluntarily agreed to assessment when applying for a job)" (APA, 2010). As a general rule, the assessment and selection programs for high-risk operational personnel of which we are aware routinely solicit informed consent from applicants, as this ensures compliance with other ethical mandates such as informing individuals about the limits of the confidentiality and the control and release of information.

In operational assessments, informed consent should include an explanation of the nature and purpose of the assessment procedures and differentiate them from the more routine or typical assessment procedures used by psychologists in health care settings. The consent form should also make clear to the applicant that the psychologist is an agent of the organization or system with a responsibility for contributing a *component* of the applicant's psychological overall suitability for a given position. It should also emphasize that participation in the assessment is voluntary and that participation can be terminated at any time. The consent form should describe the consequences of terminating the evaluation. Ideally, the consent form should detail the content of the evaluation in terms that the individual can understand. In addition, the consent form should describe how and to whom the results will be released, how the data will be stored, and whether the test results will be used for program evaluation or outcome research. As stated earlier, the consent form must also make clear the limits on confidentiality, whether the results will be shared with the individual, as well as information detailing the applicable conditions (laws or other institutional regulations) that mandate release of certain types of information without the individual's consent, such as instances of suspected child abuse or harm to others.

RESPONSIBLE PRACTICES IN THE ASSESSMENT AND SELECTION OF HIGH-RISK OPERATIONAL PERSONNEL

Psychologists have both a legal and ethical obligation to ensure that assessment and selection processes are fair, unbiased, and valid. Ethical Standard 3.01 (Unfair Discrimination) requires that "in their work-related activities, psychologists do not engage in unfair discrimination based on age, gender, gender identity, race, ethnicity, culture, national origin, religion, sexual orientation, disability, socioeconomic status, or any basis proscribed by law" (APA, 2010). This responsibility extends beyond the psychological evaluation process to include other aspects of the selection program to which the psychologist may have input, for example, the development or evaluation of scenarios or tasks that are used to evaluate essential attributes of personnel for high-risk occupations. Legal precedents suggest that interviews and other selection procedures are subject to the same standards as formal paper-and-pencil instruments (Rudner, 1992).

The responsible practice of assessment and selection of high-risk operational personnel should conform to the Uniform Guidelines on Employee Selection Procedures (1978) regardless of whether these guidelines apply to the organization or setting of the selection program. These guidelines have been adopted by the EEOC, the Civil Service Commission, the U.S. Department of Labor, and the U.S. Department of Justice and have been constructed with attention to relevant court decisions as well as to the standards of the psychological profession. The intent of the guidelines is to provide a framework for ensuring that use of tests and other employment selection procedures does not discriminate on the grounds of race, color, religion, sex, or national origin.

According to the guidelines, the use of any selection procedure that has an adverse impact on members of any race, sex, or ethnic group is considered discriminatory. Adverse impact is operationalized by the four-fifths rule. According to this rule, a selection rate for any protected group that is less than 80% of that for the group with the highest selection rate will be regarded as evidence of adverse impact unless the procedure has been validated. The guidelines detail both general and technical standards for establishing validity of selection procedures. Importantly, if the overall selection process has been shown to have an adverse impact, then all of the individual components of the selection process must be evaluated for evidence of adverse impact. Notably, if the overall selection process does not demonstrate evidence of adverse impact, then there is no requirement to evaluate the individual components for adverse impact or even to validate the individual components.

Nevertheless, the Ethics Code requires operational psychologists to use only procedures with demonstrated evidence of validity for the purpose intended. In addition, operational psychologists have an ethical obligation to ensure that other facets of the selection program are fair and unbiased and should strive to evaluate the appropriateness of those procedures, especially with regard to reliability and validity.

For example, operational psychologists can assist in the development of rating scales for assessment scenarios and tasks, educate selection personnel about issues impacting rater reliability, and assist in the evaluation of the reliability and validity of selection tasks. In short, operational psychologists who participate in the assessment and selection of high-stress operational personnel should use their expertise to ensure that the overall selection program is valid.

Detailed discussion of the processes and procedures for validating selection methods is beyond the scope of this chapter. However, operational psychologists engaged in the assessment and selection of high-risk operational personnel should be familiar with the Uniform Guidelines on Employee Selection Procedures (1978) as well as the *Principles for the Validation and Use of Personnel Selection Procedures* developed by the Society for Industrial and Organizational Psychology (2003). These principles

> specify established scientific findings and generally accepted professional practice in the field of personnel selection psychology in the choice, development, evaluation, and use of personnel selection procedures designed to measure constructs related to work behavior with a focus on the accuracy of the inferences that underlie employment decisions. (p. 1)

RECOMMENDATIONS FOR THE PROFESSIONALLY RESPONSIBLE PRACTICE OF ASSESSMENT AND SELECTION OF HIGH-RISK OPERATIONAL PERSONNEL

On the basis of the foregoing discussion, we offer in this section some minimal guidelines for the legal and ethical practice of assessment and selection of high-risk operational personnel. Our recommendations are informed by the guidelines developed by the Police Psychology Section of the International Association of Chiefs of Police (IACP) for the professional practice of preemployment psychological evaluations within the law enforcement community (IACP Police Psychological Services Section, 2005). These guidelines give 22 recommendations that form a comprehensive framework for preemployment psychological evaluations for police officers. However, most also directly apply to other occupational assessments and are easily adapted to the practice of assessing and selecting high-risk operational personnel. Informed by those guidelines, we offer recommendations for the responsible practice of assessment and selection in high-risk operational programs.

1. Operational psychologists should be familiar with and adhere to applicable federal legislation and departmental or agency directives and policies relevant to the assessment and selection of high-risk operational personnel in the settings in which they practice. Operational psychologists should adhere to the APA Ethics Code and the recent recommendations provided by the Presidential Task Force on Psychological Ethics and National Security that pertain to their roles in the assessment and selection process (see Appendix).

2. Only psychologists with training or experience in personnel selection in operational settings and psychological test interpretation with operational personnel should conduct assessments of personnel for high-risk operational positions. Operational psychologists should seek consultation from other psychologists or specialists in areas of personnel assessment and selection in which operational psychologists lack sufficient professional training or competence. Such areas might include formal job analyses, methods of establishing criterion and predictive validity, and multicultural assessment.

3. Operational psychologists conducting assessment and selection in operational programs should clarify their roles with program managers and personnel to ensure reasonable expectations. Operational psychologists should limit their roles to professional psychology activities and should not engage in other roles in the assessment program (e.g., role-player in a scenario) to avoid confusing applicants. This is especially important in selection programs in which the psychologist provides a psychological safety or oversight role in the program and may have to intervene with an applicant. In short, any interaction with an applicant in an operational assessment and selection program should be from the standpoint of a professional psychologist and limited to professional psychology activities.

4. Prior to the initiation of any psychological selection procedures, the applicant should sign an informed consent detailing, among

other things, the conditions of the evaluation, the limits of confidentiality, and the control and release of information.

5. Operational psychologists conducting assessment and selection procedures for high-risk operational personnel should identify essential psychological attributes for successful performance of duties for the population being assessed. Ideally, these should follow from job analyses. Operational psychologists must be cautious about inferring attributes from the literature or on the basis of related jobs and should take steps to ensure the generalizability of these inferences to the positions in their program.

6. Assessment and selection programs for high-risk operational personnel should include "multi-form procedures" (Fiske et al., 1948/1997) with adequate redundancy in the measurement of constructs to ensure consistency. Operational psychologists should use only reliable and valid psychological measures. Ratings developed for interviews or assessment scenarios or tasks should demonstrate adequate reliability and validity.

7. Operational psychologists should provide written reports of their suitability evaluations for each applicant. The report should summarize data from interviews, tests, and other measures used in the assessment process to support a suitability rating along with discussion of any limitations in the evaluation process or ratings.

8. Operational psychologists should take reasonable steps to ensure that all procedures used in the selection program are fair, unbiased, and valid. As such, operational psychologists should endeavor to
   - use their expertise to assist assessment and selection program staff to evaluate the psychometric properties of all instruments and measures used in the process;
   - educate assessment and selection staff about the strengths and limitations of all procedures used;
   - strive to establish a process of program evaluation in their assessment and selection programs;
   - demonstrate the validity of the process using relevant outcome criteria; and
   - conduct periodic evaluations to ensure continued reliability and validity of the procedures, including adverse impact analyses to ensure fairness.

9. As a result of security concerns in assessment and selection programs for high-risk operational personnel, there is a tendency for such programs to be highly compartmented. As a consequence, there is a risk that these assessment programs can become too insular and the process can drift into highly idiosyncratic

approaches that lack validity. When routine inspection of these programs is not required by agency directive or regulation, we recommend that operational psychologists invite other psychologists with experience in the assessment of high-risk operational personnel to review their assessment processes to ensure adherence to responsible standards of practice in the field.

CONCLUSION

The assessment and selection of high-risk operational personnel present operational psychologists with legal and ethical challenges similar to those confronted by psychologists who engage in the assessment and selection of emergency services personnel, such as police officers, or other high-reliability occupations, such as nuclear power plant employees and airline pilots. However, the unique contexts and settings for assessing and selecting high-risk operational personnel present additional ethical challenges. Many programs are situated within the U.S. Department of Defense or other federal agencies typically exempted from applicable federal legislation and regulated predominantly by agency and departmental regulations, policies, and directives. The organizational and security needs of these institutions may place operational psychologists in assessment and selection programs in direct conflict with their professional ethics. In addition, these programs tend to be extremely sensitive and compartmented, thus limiting the extent to which operational psychologists can seek consultation from peers on thorny ethical issues. Nevertheless, the ethical obligations remain the same for all psychologists regardless of the settings or roles in which they are working.

Operational psychologists must continue to identify and consider these important ethical factors, leveraging and generalizing from the experiences of others who have faced similar challenges (e.g., police psychologists). Only through sound ethical judgment and reasoning, to include peer review and consultation, can operational psychologists continue to grow as a subdiscipline and embrace an ethical practice of assessment and selection in operational settings.

REFERENCES

American Psychological Association. (1999). *Standards for educational and psychological testing.* Washington, DC: Author.

American Psychological Association. (2010). *Ethical principles of psychologists and code of conduct (2002, Amended June 1, 2010).* Retrieved from http://www.apa.org/ethics/code/index.aspx

American Psychological Association, Ethics Committee. (1993). Report of the Ethics Committee, 1993. *American Psychologist, 49,* 659–666. (Also available from http://psycnet.apa.org/journals/amp/49/7/659.pdf)

Americans With Disabilities Act of 1990, 42 U.S.C.A. § 12101 *et seq.* (West 1993).

Bush, S. S., Connell, M. A., & Denney, R. L. (2006). *Ethical practice in forensic psychology: A systematic model for decision making.* Washington, DC: American Psychological Association.

Butcher, J. N., Dahlstrom, W. G., Graham, J. R., Tellegen, A., & Kaemmer, B. (1989). *Minnesota Multiphasic Personality Inventory—2 (MMPI–2): Manual for administration and scoring.* Minneapolis: University of Minnesota Press.

Camera, W. J., & Merenda, P. F. (2000). Using personality tests in pre-employment screening: Issues raised in *Soroka v. Dayton Hudson Corporation. Psychology, Public Policy, and Law, 6,* 1164–1186.

Cattell, R. B., Cattell, A. K., & Cattell, H. E. P. (1993). *16 Personality factors fifth edition questionnaire.* Champaign, IL: Institute for Personality and Ability Testing.

Civil Service Reform Act of 1978, 5 U.S.C. 7201.

Civil Rights Act of 1991, 42 U.S.C. 1981a.

Costa, P. T., & McCrae, R. (1998). *Manual for the NEO-4.* Odessa, FL: Psychological Assessment Resources, Inc.

Enforcement Guidance: Preemployment Disability-Related Questions and Medical Examinations at 4, 8 FEP Manual (BNA) 405:7192, ff. (1995).

Ewing, C., & Gelles, M. (2003). Ethical concerns in forensic consultation regarding national safety and security. *Journal of Threat Assessment, 2,* 95–107.

Fiske, D. W., Hanfmann, E., Mackinnon, D. W., Miller, J. G., & Murray, H. A. (1997) *Selection of personnel for clandestine operations: Assessment of men.* Laguna Hills, CA: Aegean Park Press. (Original work published 1948)

Flanagan, C. L. (1995) Legal issues regarding police psychology. In M. I. Kurke & E. M. Scrivner (Eds.), *Police psychology into the 21st century* (pp. 93–107). Hillsdale, NJ: Erlbaum.

Flin, R. (2001). Selecting the right stuff: Personality and high-reliability occupations. In B. W. Roberts & R. Hogan (Eds.), *Personality psychology in the workplace.* Washington, DC: American Psychological Association.

Freedom of Information Act of 1996, 5 U.S.C. § 552, As Amended By Public Law No. 104-231, 110 Stat. 3048.

Guion, R., & Gottier, R. (1965). Validity of personality measures in personnel selection. *Personnel Psychology, 18,* 135–164.

Health Insurance Portability and Accountability Act of 1996 (HIPAA), Public Law 104-191.

International Association of Chiefs of Police, Police Psychological Services Section. (2005). Guidelines for police psychological services. *The Police Chief, 72*(9), 68–86.

Jeffrey, T. B., Rankin, R. J., & Jeffrey, L. K. (1992). In service of two masters: The ethical–legal dilemma faced by military psychologists. *Professional Psychology: Research and Practice, 23*, 91–95.

Johnson, W. B. (1995). Perennial ethical quandaries in military psychology: Toward American Psychological Association–Department of Defense collaboration. *Professional Psychology: Research and Practice, 26*, 281–287.

Johnson, W. B. (2002). Consultation in the military context: Implications of the revised training principles. *Consulting Psychology Journal: Practice and Research, 54*, 233–241.

Karraker v. Rent-A-Center, Inc., 411 F.3d 831 (7th Cir. 2005).

Kwaske, I. H. (2004). Individual assessments for personnel selection: An update on a rarely researched but avidly practiced practice. *Consulting Psychology Journal: Practice and Research, 56*, 186–195.

London, M., & Bray, D. W. (1980). Ethical issues in testing for personnel decisions. *American Psychologist, 35*, 890–901.

Lowman, R. L. (1998). *The ethical practice of psychology in organizations.* Washington, DC: American Psychological Association.

Lumsden, M. A., Bore, M., Millar, K., Jack, R., & Powis, D. (2005) Assessment of personal qualities in relation to admission to medical school. *Medical Education, 39*, 258–265.

Meyer, G., Finn, S., Eyde, L., Kay, G., Moreland, K., Dies, R., et al. (2001). Psychological testing and psychological assessment. *American Psychologist, 56*, 128–165.

Moreland, K., Eyde, L., Robertson, G., Primoff, E., & Most, R. (1995). Assessment of test user qualifications: A research-based measurement procedure. *American Psychologist, 50*, 14–23.

Picano, J. J., Williams, T. J., & Roland, R. R. (2006). Assessment and selection of high-risk operational personnel. In C. H. Kennedy & E. A. Zillmer (Eds.), *Military psychology: Clinical and operational applications* (pp. 353–370). New York: Guilford Press.

Rudner, L. M. (1992). Pre-employment testing and employee productivity. *Public Personnel Management, 21*, 133–150.

Sackett, P., Burris, L., & Callahan, C. (1989). Integrity testing for personnel selection: An update. *Personnel Psychology, 42*, 491–529.

Sampson, R. T., & Lyons, E. J. (1990). Recent legal developments in assessment and selection. *Forensic Reports, 3*, 205–223.

Society of Industrial and Organizational Psychology. (2003). *Principles for the validations and use of personnel selection procedures* (4th ed.). Bowling Green, OH: Author.

Soroka v. Dayton Hudson Corporation, 235 Cal. App. 3d 654 (1991).

Spychalski, A. (2003). *Impact of the new APA code on the use of psychological and psychiatric data in the federal government.* Retrieved January 29, 2007, from http://www.siop.org/tip/backissues/July03/08spychalsi.aspx

Staal, M. A., & Stephenson, J. A. (2006). Operational psychology: An emerging sub-discipline. *Military Psychology, 18,* 269–282.

Tippins, N. (2002). The Americans With Disabilities Act and employment testing. In R. B. Ekstrom & D. K. Smith (Eds.), *Assessing individuals with disabilities in educational, employment, and counseling settings* (pp.221–233). Washington, DC: American Psychological Association.

Uniform Guidelines on Employee Selection Procedures. (1978). 29 C.F.R. 1607. Retrieved January 30, 2007, from http://www.access.gpo.gov/nara/cfr/waisidx_07/29cfr1607_07.html

Williams, T. J., & Johnson, W. B. (2006). Introduction to the special issue: Operational psychology and clinical practice in operational environments. *Military Psychology, 18,* 261–268.

Williams, T. J., Picano, J. J., Roland, R. R., & Banks, L. M. (2006). Introduction to operational psychology. In C. H. Kennedy & E. A. Zillmer (Eds.), *Military psychology: Clinical and operational applications* (pp. 193–214). New York: Guilford Press.

3

ETHICAL CONSIDERATIONS IN THE CONDUCT OF SECURITY CLEARANCE EVALUATIONS

JAMES YOUNG, SALLY HARVEY, AND MARK A. STAAL

The number of U.S. citizens requiring a security clearance as a condition for employment runs into the millions (e.g., members of the military, certain civilians working with the military, some members of government). As one might expect, following the attacks of September 11, 2001 (9/11), the number of such jobs requiring security clearances skyrocketed. The Office of Personnel Management (OPM) estimates that nearly a million clearance requests are generated each year, and this demand has resulted in a backlog currently numbering well into the thousands. The security clearance process is designed to screen out individuals who are untrustworthy, unreliable, unable to protect classified information, or not loyal to the United States. The challenges inherent in efforts to predict individual behavior and protect the nation's secrets from espionage are compounded by today's dynamic environment, one fraught with an evolving threat as well as a shifting balance between ally and adversary.

After providing an outline of security clearance procedures, in this chapter we focus on the specific roles played by psychologists and other mental

The opinions contained in this chapter are the views of the authors and do not represent those of the U.S. Department of Defense, U.S. Department of the Army, U.S. Department of the Air Force, or the U.S. Special Operations Command.

health professionals in this investigative process as well as some of the potential ethical dilemmas that may be encountered. Additionally, we provide suggestions regarding ways in which psychologists might approach these challenges.

REQUIREMENTS AND TYPES OF SECURITY CLEARANCES

In general, security clearances are required in positions in which access to information has been restricted by the federal government. A common misperception is that only spies or individuals working in the intelligence field require security clearances. The fact is that anyone with access to classified data or equipment (e.g., aircraft in the research and development phase) requires a security clearance at least to the level at which the data or materiel is classified. For this reason, jobs requiring clearances are wide-ranging, from logistics and aviation to engineering and information technology. Security clearances are also required for individuals seeking employment in secure facilities (e.g., sensitive compartmented information facilities) or those seeking access to the nuclear weapons program.

Clearances are generally granted at a particular level, providing an individual with access to a specific type of classified information. For example, within the military community there are three levels of access (see Exhibit 3.1), and the most common levels are Secret and Top Secret (TS), both of which take a significant amount of time to acquire.

A Secret clearance can take up to 1 year to fully investigate, depending on the individual's background and activities. The investigation for individuals requiring a TS clearance, one that affords access to data that affect national security, information related to counterterrorism and counterintelligence, or other highly sensitive data, is an even more stringent process and frequently requires 18 to 24 months to complete. Having lived or traveled in multiple locations or in foreign countries as well as having relatives or close associates who reside outside the United States increases the length of the investigation, as does a history of financial difficulties or legal problems. A Secret clearance must be renewed every 10 years; a TS clearance is renewed every 5 years (U.S. Department of Defense [DoD], 1987).

EXHIBIT 3.1
Access to Sensitive Information

Confidential: The unauthorized disclosure of information or material could reasonably be expected to cause *damage* to the national security.
Secret: The unauthorized disclosure of information or material could reasonably be expected to cause *serious damage* to the national security.
Top Secret: The unauthorized disclosure of information or material could reasonably be expected to cause exceptionally *grave damage* to the national security.

Although not considered another level of clearance, there is a different type of access that allows contact with particularly sensitive information termed *Sensitive Compartmented Information* (SCI). Additionally, certain government departments may establish Special Access Programs (SAP) based on a determination regarding the exceptional vulnerability of specific information. It is assumed that the normal criteria for determining eligibility for access are insufficient to protect this material from unauthorized disclosure. In these cases, a clearance alone (e.g., TS) is normally not sufficient to gain access; the organization must also determine that there is a *need to know* the classified material. In addition to SAP, there are specific programs within the DoD requiring specialized access and evaluation, such as the Personnel Reliability Program (PRP). The PRP is a U.S. DoD program that safeguards against personnel security and safety violations associated with access to the nuclear weapons program. Members of the government with special access to nuclear weapons systems are also subject to mental health review and evaluation (U.S. DoD, 2006). Because of this program's demand for such high levels of member scrutiny, mental health providers working with PRP members find themselves in a challenging multirole relationship (i.e., treating clinician and PRP evaluator). The practitioner is faced with a difficult balancing act: as a clinician trying to foster open communication about the patient's issues and associated symptoms and as a competent medical authority for the PRP staying vigilant for issues or symptoms that are required to be reported to the patient's commander as potentially disqualifying information (i.e., information that may temporarily or permanently preclude this patient's continued access to the program). As one might imagine, maintaining a therapeutic alliance can, at times, be a significant challenge. Within the military, another issue is that often these therapeutic relationships are at overseas or isolated or rural locations where off-base or off-post mental health resources are minimal at best. How does one balance the need to report potentially disqualifying information with the need to maintain an effective therapeutic alliance, especially in the case in which there is a strong possibility that such a disclosure will lead to the patient's disapproval and potential termination of treatment in an environment where the possibility of seeking help elsewhere is limited? This and other ethical challenges are discussed later in the chapter.

LIFE CYCLE OF A SECURITY CLEARANCE

The first step in the security clearance process involves completion of the Standard Form 86 (SF-86; U.S. OPM, 2008), a document that asks for disclosure of a wide range of personal data, including current and previous residences, schools attended, employment activities, people who know the applicant well, information about the applicant's spouse and relatives, foreign travel and activities (e.g., business endeavors), criminal record, drug use, and financial information. The cover sheet for the SF-86 provides an overview of the investigatory process and includes information regarding the release of information. The applicant learns that information obtained during the investigative process will be used for the purpose of the security clearance investigation and that the Federal Privacy Act of 1974 governs any ensuing disclosure of the information, which does not require additional consent from the applicant. The last two pages of the SF-86 are a general authorization for release of information and an authorization for release of medical information, both to be signed by the applicant.

After the SF-86 (U.S. OPM, 2008) is completed, an investigation is initiated. The level of the security clearance required for the position dictates the depth of the investigation. For example, a National Agency Check with Local Agency Check (NACLAC) with credit check is required for a Secret clearance, whereas a Single Scope Background Investigation is required for TS and SCI access. Standard elements of this process involve checks of employment; education; organizational affiliations; areas where the person has lived, worked, or gone to school; and interviews with those who know the individual— employers, coworkers, friends, and other associates (U.S. DoD, 1987). The investigation may include a NACLAC on the applicant's spouse and any immediate family members who were not born as U.S. citizens. Some positions (e.g., National Security Agency, Central Intelligence Agency) also require a polygraph examination (U.S. DoD, 1985).

Once the investigation is complete, the information enters the adjudication phase. The main concerns of the adjudication process are twofold: (a) to identify any conflicts of interest that could cause an individual to choose between commitments to the United States and another compelling loyalty; and (b) to determine a person's reliability, trustworthiness, and ability to protect classified information as demonstrated by the facts of a person's life.

> The adjudicative process is an examination of a sufficient period of a person's life to make an affirmative determination that the person is an acceptable security risk. Eligibility for access to classified information is predicated upon the individual meeting these personnel security guidelines. The adjudication process is the careful weighing of a number of variables known as the whole-person concept. Available, reliable information about the person, past and present, favorable and unfavorable, should be considered in reaching a determination. (Hadley, 2005, p. 2)

The *Adjudicative Guidelines for Determining Eligibility for Access to Classified Information* (approved by President George W. Bush, December 29, 2005; Hadley, 2005) require that *common sense judgment* be used in determining whether someone will be granted a security clearance. Specifically, the evaluator will assess the person by considering the following 13 guidelines:

Guideline A: Allegiance to the United States,
Guideline B: Foreign Influence,
Guideline C: Foreign Preference,
Guideline D: Sexual Behavior,
Guideline E: Personal Conduct,
Guideline F: Financial Considerations,
Guideline G: Alcohol Consumption,
Guideline H: Drug Involvement,
Guideline I: Psychological Conditions,
Guideline J: Criminal Conduct,
Guideline K: Handling Protected Information,
Guideline L: Outside Activities, and
Guideline M: Use of Information Technology Systems.

The following factors are considered in weighing the relevance of an individual's conduct: (a) the nature, extent, and seriousness of the conduct; (b) the circumstances surrounding the conduct, including knowledgeable participation; (c) the frequency and recency of the conduct; (d) the individual's age and maturity at the time of the conduct; (e) the extent to which the participation is voluntary; (f) the presence or absence of rehabilitation and other permanent behavioral changes; (g) the motivation for the conduct; (h) the potential for pressure, coercion, exploitation, or duress; and (i) the likelihood of continuance or recurrence.

It is probably obvious that several of these categories involve areas that fall into the mental health practitioner's area of expertise (e.g., psychological conditions, drug abuse and addiction, alcohol consumption, sexual behavior). As we discuss in the next section, the role of the mental health professional is not insignificant, and often his or her evaluation is vital to the overall process of making the most appropriate decision regarding security risk.

ROLE OF THE MENTAL HEALTH PROVIDER

Mental health providers can become involved in this process at several junctures: (a) within the investigation process, (b) during the adjudication phase, (c) during one of many periodic reviews, and (d) following an incidental disclosure of a violation. The first point involves situations in which the individual seeking a clearance has received treatment, including substance abuse services. As the process currently stands, the SF-86 (U.S. OPM, 2008) asks applicants several questions that relate to psychiatric treatment. For example, applicants indicate whether they have consulted with a mental health professional within the last 7 years and if so, to disclose the dates of treatment and the name and address of the treating clinician. In the event that the treatment involved "only marital, family or grief counseling, not related to violence by you," disclosure of the treatment dates and therapist information is not required (U.S. OPM, 2008). In a related section, the applicant is asked if use of alcohol has resulted in any alcohol-related treatment or counseling over the past 7 years. Again, if affirmative, the applicant must supply the dates of treatment, identity of the clinician, and related contact information. It should be noted that recent developments within the U.S. DoD have reduced the reporting obligations on members who have been seen by mental health providers if those visitations were combat related. Moreover, Secretary of Defense Robert Gates specifically cited Question 21 from the SF-86 security questionnaire, which asks applicants whether they have ever received treatment for mental health issues, in his directed policy changes. Secretary Gates indicated that he was attempting to balance the troops' needs to get help with those of the intelligence community. Accordingly, the revised SF 86 question directs respondents to answer "no" to Question 21 if the care was "strictly related to adjustments from service in a military combat environment." This policy change was directed by Secretary Gates on April 18, 2008, and it is as yet unclear what second- or third-order effects may arise as a result of this new approach. Clearly one hope expressed by the Undersecretary for Intelligence James R. Clapper and the Undersecretary for Personnel and Readiness David Chu is that "seeking professional care for these mental health issues should not be perceived to jeopardize an individual's security clearance" (Miles, 2008).

As previously indicated, when completing the SF-86, the applicant is also asked to sign an "Authorization for Release of Medical Information." This authorization allows the investigator to obtain responses to the following three questions involving mental health consultations (U.S. OPM, 2008):

1. Does the person under investigation have a condition or treatment that could impair his or her judgment or reliability particularly in the context of safeguarding classified national security information or special nuclear information or material?
2. If so, please describe the nature of the condition and the extent and duration of the impairment and/or treatment.
3. What is the prognosis?

At the time of the interview with the applicant, the receipt of mental health treatment is verified, and the investigator asks that a second release be signed— Specific Release OFI-16A (U.S. OPM, 1989). This document authorizes the investigator to obtain specific clinical information regarding the applicant, including "but not limited to: dates of confinement, participation or treatment;

diagnosis; doctors' orders; medication sheets; urine result reports; prognosis; and medical opinions regarding my health, recovery and/or rehabilitation," (U.S. OPM, 1989) and allows for other information to be released as requested by the applicant. In the event that an applicant has received mental health treatment outside the identified exclusion (i.e., marital, family, grief), the investigator will attempt to contact the provider and obtain responses to these questions.

The second juncture at which assistance from a mental health provider can be sought occurs during the adjudication phase. After reviewing the information compiled during the course of the investigation, an adjudicator may require that a specialized evaluation be performed to assess the applicant's security risk. This often occurs when there is a positive response from a treating provider indicating that the applicant does have a condition potentially impacting his or her ability to safeguard information. However, evidence of impaired judgment, questionable reliability, or heightened risk of violent or irregular behavior is also likely to trigger a request for additional information. Specialized mental health evaluations also result when the treating providers are unable to address those questions or indicate that they have "no opinion." Although beyond the scope of this chapter, the interested reader is directed to U.S. DoD Directive 6490.1 (U.S. DoD, 1997a) and U.S. DoD Instruction 6490.4 (U.S. DoD, 1997b) for further information on the implementation of command directed mental health evaluations (see also Budd & Harvey, 2006).

An important consideration for these evaluations is that they are not intended as punitive in nature but rather are requested to help make a determination and/or to clarify psychological issues related to judgment and reliability. Because a positive benefit is not intended, the role of the psychologist is more forensic in nature with the *client,* the organization, seeking to protect sensitive programs and information. For this reason, it should be noted that such evaluations and the security-related risk assessments associated with them can create specific ethical challenges. For example, in many situations there may only be one mental health provider available at a given military base or post to conduct both the security (and possibly the follow-on command-directed mental health evaluation) and the mental health care functions. In these instances, the risk of multiple relationships is great, and various mitigation strategies are recommended. These strategies are discussed in greater detail later in the chapter.

The third instance in which a mental health provider might engage in security clearance consultation can occur during one of the many periodic reviews or reinvestigations conducted while the member holds his or her clearance. As stated earlier, those holding TS clearances require a periodic reinvestigation every 5 years. For those individuals conducting more sensitive duties (part of SAP or working with nuclear weapons programs as part of the PRP), the frequency of follow-on review may be greater. In such cases, members are often brought in for a medical records review and psychological interview. As one can imagine, various life events might occur after the time at which the individual's initial clearance was granted that could be cause for concern (e.g., divorce, drunk-driving charges, other legal infractions, financial difficulties). Periodic re-investigations and their corresponding psychological evaluations help ensure continued monitoring and support for such difficulties.

Finally, mental health providers occasionally come across incidental disclosures of potential security-related violations or potentially disqualifying information. These disclosures can occur within the context of psychotherapy as well as under other circumstances (e.g., social). Mental health providers working in a remote or small base or post environment have been routinely compared with providers in rural settings where their professional duties and affiliations often comingle with their personal and social ones (Staal & King, 2000). In such environments it is very difficult to eliminate all multiple relationships, increasing the likelihood of such disclosures. In the case of the patient, the ethical dilemma is clear, how can the mental health provider separate allegiances to both the individual and the organization? On one hand there exists an obligation to facilitate a "safe" environment in which the provider's patient can feel free to talk openly about concerns and issues. On the other hand, mental health providers have clear directives as military members to report any violations in regulations or laws or other potentially disqualifying information (e.g., a noteworthy symptom) that is disclosed, including those that might lead to a negative impact on their security clearance. Unfortunately, in doing so, these providers jeopardize the therapeutic relationship they have with their patient. Although there are several ways to mitigate this risk and balance the allegiance to two masters (American Psychological Association [APA], Presidential Task Force on Psychological Ethics and National Security, 2005; Jeffrey, Rankin, & Jeffrey, 1992), one of the best ways is to lean heavily on informed consent (APA, 2010). This course of action is discussed further in a later section of the chapter.

SECURITY CLEARANCE EVALUATIONS

What are some examples of the types of psychiatric issues that might give an evaluator reason to be concerned about an individual's trustworthiness or reliability? According to the adjudicative guidelines,

> certain emotional, mental and personality conditions can impair judgment, reliability or trustworthiness. The guidelines do not require a formal diagnosis of a disorder for there to be a concern. A qualified mental health

professional (e.g., clinical psychologist or psychiatrist) employed by, or acceptable to and approved by the US Government, should be consulted when evaluating potentially disqualifying and mitigating information under this guideline. (Hadley, 2005)

For example, sexual behavior that is difficult to control and considered self-destructive and high risk may be disqualifying. In particular, one would attend to behavior that might reflect psychological instability, demonstrate poor judgment, or increase a person's vulnerability to coercion or exploitation. Another example might be excessive alcohol consumption, potentially leading certain individuals to have poor impulse control or demonstrate questionable judgment. To the extent that a person is unable to control his or her behavior because of alcohol consumption or the need for alcohol, one has good reason to be concerned about his or her reliability. Additionally, substance abuse can lead to organic-based cognitive dysfunction that decreases the probability of understanding, remembering, or consistently complying with security procedures and policies. Excessive use of alcohol, irrespective of whether that behavior is classified as *abuse* or *dependence* may be disqualifying, although positive changes to behavior supportive of sobriety can be a mitigating factor.

What about anxiety disorders? A concern with those suffering from anxiety spectrum disorders might be that the individual is sufficiently preoccupied that security procedures are not appropriately attended to. In this case, rather than a willful violation of security procedures, one might unintentionally violate such practices because of the distracting effects of anxiety or his or her anxiety-related thoughts. Of course, any psychological disorder (e.g., schizophrenia, delusional disorder) that is an assault on the integrity of the person's thought processes would most likely diminish his or her ability to comprehend and adhere to security procedures.

Undesirable character traits constitute another personnel security criterion. For example, a narcissistic personality may lead to security violations fueled by a certain degree of entitlement. The more one assumes being above the law, beyond common policies and procedures, and unbound by convention, the more one may choose not to protect classified information. With the narcissist, there may also be a strong desire to demonstrate one's importance or indulge one's ego by interacting with high-level representatives of a foreign government. The atmosphere of secrecy may fuel these delusions of grandeur. Someone with a dependent personality may be vulnerable to exploitation by those who offer to satisfy deep-seated needs for affiliation, nurturance, and security.

Another personal security criterion is an individual's financial profile. Historically, financial problems have been implicated in several known cases of espionage (Herbig, 2008). The crucial issues are not the objective amount of debt or, for that matter, the size of one's nest egg. Instead, the underlying issue is the psychological meaning of money—greed, need for power, sense of entitlement, preoccupations, and the love of and strong need to provide for one's family. A history of gambling addiction would also raise significant concerns. This addiction may create a financial situation that tempts an individual to seek illegal sources of income, or it might make them more vulnerable to coercion or blackmail.

Although there are many potentially disqualifying issues, there is clearly no cookbook of inevitable linkages (Bloom, 1993). Instead, the insightfulness and acumen of the assessor are vital. A security clearance evaluation should be as thorough as possible, including not only psychological testing but also a review of medical, personnel, and background investigative information. Anyone charged with conducting these evaluations is likely to ask what is known about the criteria used to predict the behavior evaluators are attempting to select out (e.g., unreliability, poor judgment, inadvertent release of information, and espionage).

With regard to espionage, there have been several studies that arose following a spike in the number of American spies arrested during the 1980s. The Stillwell Commission called for a more scientific study of espionage (U.S. DoD, Commission to Review DoD Security Policy and Practices, 1985). One of those efforts, spearheaded by the Defense Personnel Security Research Center (U.S. DoD, 1992), resulted in the development of a database designed to develop a deeper understanding of the factors that lead an individual to commit espionage. The most recent publication from this organization investigated the biographic attributes, employment factors, motivations, and consequences for 173 people and their acts of completed or attempted espionage committed between 1947 and 2007 (Herbig, 2008). The researchers divided the group into the following three cohorts: 1947–1979, 1980–1989, and 1990–2007. In addition to various demographic information (e.g., gender, race or ethnicity, education, marital status, age when espionage began, native-born vs. naturalized citizens, military vs. civilians, level of clearance), they provided a discussion of variables that were determined to be the motivators for espionage activities. For example, looking historically, it was determined that money has become less important as a motivator. Financial gain was a motivator for 47% of the individuals from the first cohort, 74% from the second, but only 7% for those involved in espionage from 1990 to the present. Divided loyalties and disgruntlement were additional significant motivators for espionage, and both appear to be more prevalent today than in the past. Other reasons given for involvement were the following: coercion, ingratiation, thrills, and recognition or ego. Since 1990, the number of spies indicating loyalty to a foreign government or cause more than doubled. Another finding was that 33% of those participating in espionage did so after a significant personal crisis (e.g., divorce, terminal illness of close friend or family member). Although this last finding is interesting, especially when one considers the possible link between psychological vulnerabilities and espionage, it is important to point out that for every person who participated in espionage following a personal crisis, millions of others with access to classified data did not. Because the base rate for the behavior is incredibly low, it is difficult to unravel the complexities involved in determining the motivation for such behavior.

ETHICAL CONSIDERATIONS WITH REGARD TO SECURITY CLEARANCE EVALUATIONS

Several ethical issues may arise when conducting security clearances. Some of these occur more often than others, depending on the setting (e.g., military vs. civilian, stateside or overseas, within a clinic with several other qualified clinicians vs. in isolation as the only available clinician). Although certainly not an exhaustive list, the following sections address the primary ethical dilemmas encountered in this area of practice.

Repercussions of Evaluation

Principle A: Beneficence and Nonmaleficence, of the APA Ethics Code states that "psychologists strive to benefit those with whom they work and take care to do no harm" (APA, 2010). Psychologists doing this type of work must seriously consider the long-term implications of a particular clinical opinion or recommendation. Even though evaluating mental health professionals do not have the final say and adjudications regarding suitability for a particular clearance occur on the basis of the "whole person," career trajectories can be changed and sometimes terminated on the basis of a single evaluation and recommendation if it brings clarity to identified risk factors. That is not to say that mental health professionals should shy away from providing an accurate and truthful assessment but rather that they should not render such evaluations and clinical opinions without considerable care and deliberation. As noted by Johnson (2008), military psychologists often have a tremendous amount of power over the lives of those with whom they work clinically. This is true of any mental health professional tasked with conducting these types of security evaluations.

It is essential that the obligations to the patient being evaluated are weighed as well as those to the organization requesting the assessment. Although in some ways it may be easier to implement an across-the-board assessment approach that is highly conservative, always erring on the side of caution, such an approach would add little to the process. This may be difficult to resist in a highly risk-averse environment in which the system is unable to tolerate breaches of security (analogous to suicide risk assessments, when poor predictions are made in the security, intelligence, or nuclear arenas, the outcome is usually very bad). Moreover, in adopting this posture evaluators introduce the risk of increasing the number of false positives (i.e., inaccurately making a determination of significant risk).

Multiple Roles

As mentioned previously, it would not be uncommon as a military psychologist to face the prospect of being asked to conduct a security clearance evaluation on a current patient. This request is dealt with easily in situations in which multiple mental health evaluators are present. The most common course of action in such situations is to transfer the security clearance evaluation to a different provider, separating the roles and reporting responsibilities. In this way, the APA's intent for avoiding multiple relationships (APA, 2010; Standard 3.05) is met, the potential bias associated with the conflict of interest is avoided, and the therapeutic relationship is relatively undisturbed. Unfortunately, in many instances separating roles is not possible let alone feasible. In remote or small base locations, there may only be one qualified mental health provider available. In such settings, the multiple relationship is likely unavoidable. However, there are a number of things that one can do to help mitigate the risk and reduce the negative effects to both individual patients and organizational clients. Informed consent is at the top of the list.

Mental health facilities incorporate a form of informed consent at the outset of any evaluation or treatment relationship. Such consent typically includes the contingency for future evaluations associated with legal, military, or mission requirements. In doing so, this document serves to put prospective patients on notice about the various risks and complications that might arise, such as the need to provide their command or security apparatus with input regarding their access to classified or sensitive information and/or systems. Within the military and intelligence culture these limitations are generally well understood and accepted.

In addition to securing informed consent prior to establishing the relationship, mental health providers may also choose to discuss their concerns with the patient's command element or security manager (following the evaluation request). Although these individuals may be bound by their own regulations, in some instances there is flexibility as to the nature or depth of evaluation required. Being able to tailor the evaluation and thus balance the information needs of the organization with the privacy needs of the individual may help preserve both relationships. For example, in the case of a military member being seen for past abuse (e.g., in childhood), there is likely little concern that such information would have to be revealed beyond the therapeutic relationship. In this case, this information may have no bearing on the individual's reliability or judgment concerning classified programs. Therefore, an evaluation or report that contains such personal information, passed through channels of the individual's command, would be unnecessary and inappropriate in this instance. Furthermore, clarifying the organization's specific questions and discussing the potential risks of violating the individual's privacy with his or her command can sometimes bring about a more balanced outcome.

Last, consultation with peers and colleagues cannot be emphasized enough. In real estate, the answer seems always to be "location, location, location." However, when it comes to ethical dilemmas, the mantra is no less than "consultation, consultation, consultation." Many times psychologists feel that they have run every answer to ground and feel trapped in a course of action that is undesirable. However, pulling in a third party to help mental health providers see the forest from the trees can be critical in successfully navigating such circumstances. Many psychologists have dealt with the same issues, and as a new or less experienced mental health provider, there is no sense in reinventing the wheel. The majority of mental health providers welcome the opportunity to share lessons learned.

As an example of the challenges of dual roles, imagine a case in which a mental health provider is actively engaged with a patient who reveals psychiatric symptoms that if known by his command would disqualify him or her from continued access to the nuclear weapons program. According to access guidelines, the individual holding the security clearance has an obligation to report this but has chosen not to do so. The provider understands his or her obligation to formally notify the commander but also realizes how reluctant this particular patient was to seek treatment in the first place and what a disclosure of this information might do to the patient's willingness to continue treatment. To make matters more complicated, if the mental health provider recommends temporary removal from PRP status because of the symptoms, some might argue that the provider's divided loyalties have created a therapeutic environment in which there is some pressure on the patient to get "better" in an effort to regain PRP status. What if, at the next session, the patient claims that his or her issues have resolved. If the provider believes that the patient's quick "recovery" is not legitimate, now he or she is faced with a patient who is not only experiencing psychological symptoms but also has decided to be dishonest about them. What if the provider explains his or her concerns to the patient and he or she continues to insist that the recovery is authentic? What role does the mental health provider assume? Does he or she take what the patient says at face value? Does he or she consider permanent disqualification from the PRP program on the assumption that the patient is unreliable? If so, what are the implications? To make matters slightly more complicated, what if the mental health provider is the only psychologist available at this location and the patient does not have access to another provider? These are all difficult questions, and answers to them often rely on the unique merits of each situation. However, they illustrate the potential complexity that mental health providers face in these situations.

Competence

Principle C: Integrity of the APA Ethics Code states that "Psychologists seek to promote accuracy, honesty, and truthfulness in the science, teaching, and practice of psychology" (APA, 2010). Furthermore, Standard 2.01 of the Ethics Code states that psychologists should limit their practice of psychology to areas in which they have established competence. Can a psychologist say with confidence that he or she can accurately predict the degree to which someone will lack in trustworthiness, reliability, and/or loyalty at some future time?

Unfortunately, when it comes to predicting future behavior, particularly when that behavior constitutes a low-frequency event like espionage or breaches of classified information, no one does it well. Psychologists typically throw around notions like "the best predictor of future behavior is past behavior," yet little is known about predicting future behavior. Humans are so complex and the landscape of human interaction is so diverse that it is difficult to predict with accuracy what someone is likely to do. That said, psychologists must not conclude there is nothing to offer. On the contrary, operational psychologists must be diligent in studying the specific behavior and conditions that predict reliability and fidelity and must artfully marry those to the context and requirements of the mission being considered (APA, 2010; Standard 2.04). For example, although there are many factors that are likely to overlap regardless of position or duties, there are likely to be some differences in the security requirements for one position versus another. The risk factors and attributes associated with a military member posting guard on the flight line would differ from those associated with a clandestine counterintelligence agent. Thus, the sorts of variables considered between these two groups are likely to differ as well. Moreover, these factors probably change depending on the individual circumstances under evaluation. What makes a 25-year-old single male agent susceptible to influence may differ from the susceptibilities of a married 55-year-old female agent. To evaluate the risks of these two individuals, one must understand the dynamics at play and how to assess them.

That said, very little research is available in the public domain that informs evaluators. So how is one able to fulfill the ethical responsibilities to practice within the professional scope as well as base one's work on established scientific and professional knowledge? First, mental health providers must assess their own qualifications and abilities to competently conduct such evaluations. Psychologists are likely to improve the usefulness of their security clearance evaluations and their ethical decision making by continuing to gain further experience and knowledge in this area. This can be accomplished by seeking additional assessment opportunities; establishing ongoing consultation with senior psychologists; and reading available historical case analyses of community violations, security breaches, and organizational espionage (e.g., Hadley, 2005; Herbig, 2008). Psychologists should learn what factors affecting members of the community under consideration have led to lapses in their judgment, degraded their reliability, and compromised their fidelity. These recommendations are consistent with a recognition-based decision-making model and supported by Stephenson and Staal (2007), who have argued that as the decision maker (e.g., mental health provider) gains more experience and knowledge in a particular arena, the quality of ethical decision making improves.

Privacy and Confidentiality

Ethical Standard 4.02, Discussing the Limits of Confidentiality, requires that psychologists "discuss with persons . . . and organizations with whom they establish scientific or professional relationships (1) the relevant limits of confidentiality and (2) the foreseeable uses of the information generated through their psychological activities" (APA, 2010). One can easily see how even the best informed consent and a thorough review of this consent by a treating psychologist might not result in a sufficient appreciation of the far-reaching effects of a patient's participation in treatment. For example, can psychologists realistically expect a patient presenting for depression treatment to understand that participation in such treatment might determine years down the road whether he or she is granted a particular security clearance? Examples like this underscore the importance of spending a sufficient amount of time explaining the limits of confidentiality, especially reasons that others might request information about treatment participation, prognosis, and more. Too often this informed consent process stops after the first session. A good general practice would be to continue to remind one's patients of the limits of confidentiality throughout the treatment process. Because of their mental state at the initial session, many patients are unlikely to fully grasp the informed consent procedures. Additionally, as time passes, the probability that the nuances of informed consent (e.g., limits of confidentiality) will be remembered is often minimal. Another course of action available to the provider is to contact the patient prior to releasing information. Not only does this serve as a warning enabling applicants to prepare for the outcome but in some cases it also gives the person an opportunity to withdraw his or her application for a particular position (American Psychiatric Association, 2006). This will increase the probability of maintaining a good therapeutic alliance and prevent unnecessary intrusions on the patient's privacy.

On a related note, for those mental health providers who frequently change jobs (e.g., military clinicians), it is important to be mindful of how clinical notes might be interpreted at some future date by another clinician. Often a clinical opinion or review of mental health records is requested after the treating clinician has departed. The importance of clarity in documentation is underscored by the fact that sometimes other clinicians are attempting to answer these security-related questions by interpreting another provider's notes. McCauley, Hughes, and Liebling-Kalifani (2008) noted that providers often do not have control over the future use of a patient's mental health records. On the other hand, as a clinician charged with providing information from another provider's notes, it is important to take care not to extend clinical opinions or recommendations beyond what is clearly indicated by the notes. Finally, it is always a good idea to document in the patient's chart the content and rationale of any disclosure of information and associated recommendations.

SUMMARY AND CONCLUSION

In the wake of 9/11, the need to safeguard information critical to national security has never been greater. Similarly, the role that mental health providers play in executing evaluations to ensure such fidelity has increased. Operational psychologists and other mental health providers are just one link in the consultative chain to the command authority or security service granting security clearances. Operational psychologists provide recommendations based on perceived risk but do not determine the outcome of an individual's security investigation. However, a concomitant increase in potential ethical dilemmas has also occurred with the rise in such evaluations. Therefore, decision-making models and ethical frameworks that help guide practitioners are in high demand.

Our goal in writing this chapter was to provide a brief overview of the security clearance process as well as a discussion regarding a variety of ethical dilemmas inherent in conducting security clearance evaluations. To reiterate some of these thoughts, with regard to patients, the use of rigorous informed consent procedures is recommended, as is being specific about the ways in which the information about treatment might be used at a later date. In cases in which the mental health professional is playing multiple roles, a careful prioritization of the needs of the various clients (i.e., patient or applicant and organization) is needed, as is a thoughtful consideration of the specifics of each case rather than the use of a broad-brush approach for such evaluations and recommendations. Also, as practitioners it is important to gain as much experience and knowledge in this specific domain as possible. Providers should seek new opportunities for practice, mentorship from senior mental health professionals and frequent consultation from peers and professional organizations, especially when faced with difficult ethical dilemmas.

Within the military environment, we recommend that psychologists be introduced to the practice of security clearance evaluations as early as possible, preferably during residency training. This is especially important for those who will be going from residency programs to small bases or posts where they will be the only mental health provider for that community. Last, in those cases in which clinicians are providing clinical information and/or opinions about a current or previous patient or another provider's former patient, it is important to document the rationale for and content of these disclosures.

To the degree that psychologists continue to challenge thinking and seek additional opportunities to learn about the best ways to conduct such evaluations, both security-related assessment abilities and ethical decision making surrounding these assessments will be improved.

REFERENCES

American Psychiatric Association. (2006). *Psychiatrists' responses to requests for psychiatric information in federal personnel investigations.* Retrieved May 30, 2008, from http://archive.psych.org/edu/other_res/lib_archives/archives/200602.pdf

American Psychological Association. (2010). *Ethical principles of psychologists and code of conduct (2002, Amended June 1, 2010).* Retrieved from http://www.apa.org/ethics/code/index.aspx

American Psychological Association, Presidential Task Force on Psychological Ethics and National Security. (2005). *Report of the American Psychological Association Presidential Task Force on Psychological Ethics and National Security.* Retrieved June 4, 2009, from http://www.apa.org/releases/PENSTaskForceReportFinal.pdf

Bloom, R. W. (1993). Psychological assessment for security clearances, special access, and sensitive positions. *Military Medicine, 158,* 609–613.

Budd, F. C., & Harvey, S. (2006). Military fitness-for-duty evaluations. In C. H. Kennedy & E. A. Zillmer (Eds.), *Military psychology: Clinical and operational applications.* New York: Guilford Press.

Federal Privacy Act of 1974, 5 U.S.C. § 552a(b).

Hadley, S. J. (2005). *Adjudicative guidelines for determining eligibility for access to classified information.* Retrieved May 29, 2008, http://www.fas.org/sgp/isoo/guidelines.html

Herbig, K. L. (2008). *Changes in espionage by Americans: 1947–2007* (Tech. Rep. No. 08-05). Monterey, CA: Defense Personnel Security Research.

Jeffrey, T. B., Rankin, R. J., & Jeffrey, L. K. (1992). In service of two masters: The ethical–legal dilemma faced by military psychologists. *Professional Psychology: Research and Practice, 16,* 385–397.

Johnson, W. B. (2008). Top ethical challenges for military clinical psychologists. *Military Psychology, 20*, 49–62.

McCauley, M. Hughes, J. H., & Liebling-Kalifani, H. (2008). Ethical considerations for military clinical psychologists: A review of selected literature. *Military Psychology, 20*, 7–20.

Miles, D. (2008). *Gates works to reduce mental health stigma.* Retrieved 29, May, 2008, from http://www.defenselink.mil/news/newsarticle.aspx?id=49738

Staal, M. A., & King, R. E. (2000). Managing a dual relationship environment: The ethics of military psychology. *Professional Psychology: Research and Practice, 31*, 698–705.

Stephenson, J. A., & Staal, M. A. (2007). An ethical decision-making model for operational psychology. *Ethics & Behavior, 17*, 61–82.

U.S. Department of Defense. (1985). *Polygraph program* (DOD Publication No. 5210.48-R). Washington, DC: U.S. Government Printing Office.

U.S. Department of Defense. (1987). *Personnel security program* (DODD No. 5200.2). Washington, DC: U.S. Government Printing Office.

U.S. Department of Defense. (1992). *Defense Personnel Security Research Center (PERSEREC)* (DODD No. 5201.79). Washington, DC: U.S. Government Printing Office.

U.S. Department of Defense (1997a). *Mental health evaluations of members of the Armed Forces* (DODD No. 6490.1). Washington, DC: U.S. Government Printing Office.

U.S. Department of Defense. (1997b). *Mental health evaluations of members of the Armed Forces* (DODI No. 6490.4). Washington, DC: U.S. Government Printing Office.

U.S. Department of Defense. (2006). *Nuclear weapon personnel reliability program (PRP)* (DODD No. 5210.42). Washington, DC: U.S. Government Printing Office.

U.S. Department of Defense, Commission to Review DoD Security Policy and Practices. (1985). *Keeping the nation's secrets: A report to the Secretary of Defense.* Washington, DC: U.S. Government Printing Office.

U.S. Office of Personnel Management. (1989). *Specific release* (Form No.OFI-16A. 1969-242-420/05170). Washington, DC: U.S. Government Printing Office.

U.S. Office of Personnel Management. (2008). *Questionnaire for national security positions* (Standard Form No. 86). Washington, DC: U.S. Government Printing Office.

4

ETHICAL DILEMMAS IN PSYCHOLOGICAL CONSULTATION TO COUNTERINTELLIGENCE AND COUNTERTERRORISM ACTIVITIES

KIRK KENNEDY, RANDY BORUM, AND ROBERT FEIN

Psychologists providing consultation to counterintelligence (CI) and counterterrorism (CT) missions of the U.S. Armed Forces and the U.S. Department of Defense (DoD) face multiple professional and personal challenges. The required roles and functions in operational support are quite distinct from those in providing clinical or health services, yet few guidelines or professional standards exist specifically for this area of practice. In this relatively uncharted territory, psychologists must navigate carefully to avoid the ethical pitfalls that may arise in supporting these critical but challenging missions. In this chapter, we review how DoD psychologists support CI and CT operations and investigations by summarizing Shumate and Borum (2006); then we discuss the most pertinent ethical dilemmas psychologists may encounter in these activities; and we finish by describing the ways DoD psychologists are working to resolve these ethical issues. This chapter cannot address every possible dilemma or set an ethical standard of practice. Instead, we present a broad view by examining how psychologists might apply the General Principles

The views expressed in this article are those of the authors and do not reflect the official policy or position of the U.S. Department of the Army, U.S. Department of Defense, or the U.S. Government.

of the American Psychological Association's (APA's) "Ethical Principles of Psychologists and Code of Conduct" (APA, 2010) to their consultation activities in support of CI and CT operations. The CI and CT case studies provided here are illustrative, not factual. They are fictionalized to avoid compromising classified information. When discussing examples in the ethics sections, only those unclassified aspects of the situation are mentioned. Although this may raise questions for the reader, we concluded that sharing contours of the situation was better than not sharing any information at all.

PSYCHOLOGICAL CONSULTATION TO COUNTERINTELLIGENCE AND COUNTERTERRORISM OPERATIONS: COMMON ROLES AND FUNCTIONS

A relatively small but growing number of psychologists have assumed professional roles and duties that focus primarily on supporting CI and CT operations. These psychologists are not assigned to these roles for purposes of providing health-related services and sometimes describe their role or themselves as *operational psychologists* to emphasize this distinction. These professionals primarily support operators (or case officers) and investigators by consulting about and assessing human sources of information (i.e., *assets* in the intelligence lexicon). As a result, operational psychologists are in a position to help service members and intelligence professionals understand an asset's personality and motivational and situational dynamics and to offer suggestions or guidance about the *management and control* (often referred to as *handling*) of these individuals. The handling recommendations frequently relate to psychological or behavioral issues that are relevant for planning, managing, or maintaining an operational activity. In addition, psychologists may conduct risk assessments, make recommendations on source recruitment and handling, and offer opinions on the veracity and credibility of the information sources provide. These activities provide an opportunity for psychologists to contribute in important new ways to U.S. security. These activities also present an array of questions and potential challenges to the profession of psychology as it explores the contours of these nontraditional roles.

Psychological consultation activities in support of CI and CT operations are part of a nascent specialty area often referred to either as *operational psychology* (particularly in a military context) or *national security psychology*. CI refers to

> information gathered and activities conducted to protect against espionage, other intelligence activities, sabotage, or assassinations conducted for or on behalf of foreign powers, organizations or persons or international terrorist activities, but not including personnel, physical, document or

communications security programs. (Executive Order No. 12,333, 1981, General Provisions section, para. 5)

CT operations are designed to detect, disrupt, and prevent acts of terrorism against U.S. persons, assets, and interests. Psychologists often consult to CI and CT operations on issues of risk, recruitment, handling, and other aspects of information collection. CI risk assessment questions include psychological evaluations to *screen out* or provide advice on dealing appropriately with individuals whose personality characteristics may place them at risk for security compromise or for job performance problems (Borum, Super, & Rand, 2003). These evaluations may also require assessing whether an individual has a psychological condition or impairment (e.g., anxiety or concern about the risk involved in the mission) that could compromise the operation's success and, if possible, suggesting how to contain, suppress, or manage the psychological distress through stress management skills to ensure mission objectives can be accomplished.

In consulting to recruitment operations, psychologists may be asked to assess personality, motivational, and cultural variables that may affect an individual's performance. Because cultural differences can affect the relationship's trust, clarity of communication, interpretation of behavior, delivery of instructions, and a host of other behavioral issues, the psychologist can sometimes bring a degree of objectivity or cross-cultural insight to the observations and impressions of those directly involved in the case. Once an individual is recruited, psychologists may provide consultation, assistance, and support to an operator or investigator regarding such issues as ongoing credibility assessment, problem solving, and monitoring and managing an agent's vulnerabilities and mental condition. For example, frequently there is a battle for control of the relationship between the operator and the individual reporting information of CI or CT value. It is helpful to raise the operator's awareness of this dynamic to maximize the potential for the success of the case.

Psychologists also may add value by providing training in interview and elicitation skills and asset validation and by providing cultural perspectives to assist in understanding foreign assets. In this role, psychologists may observe behavior and provide input into its interpretation as well as whether and how the asset is responding to the interviewer or particular strategy or line of questions. The psychologist may be able to provide information to the operators and other interviewers about the source's motivations, beliefs, attitudes, values, personality, cognitive functioning, memory, and social identities. Psychologists may draw on the empirical literature bearing on persuasion and interpersonal influence to suggest potential strategies for pursuing accurate and timely information. They may provide counsel on the source's motivations or help to assess his or her credibility or attempts at deception.

Psychologists also consult on counterespionage activities. Fundamentally, espionage is about stealing nation, state, or terrorist group secrets. The United States and most other nations routinely classify and safeguard certain information that is considered vital to national security. The objective is to protect information that if known to enemies, adversaries, or those with hostile intention, could expose weaknesses and vulnerabilities or mitigate a strategic advantage. Defensive counterespionage activities are designed to thwart the efforts of those seeking to steal U.S. secrets or to use them for unauthorized purposes. Offensive counterespionage operations seek to recruit individuals who have access to others' secrets.

Members of any foreign intelligence service (FIS) are presumed to be hostile to U.S. security interests; it is sometimes said that there are friendly nations but no friendly intelligence services (Olson, 2001). For the FIS or hostile nonstate faction looking to infiltrate or compromise the United States, in many cases, the most direct way for them to steal U.S. secrets is to get them from someone who has legitimate access (National Security Agency, 2001). This raises one of the most serious and vexing problems in contemporary counterespionage, the insider threat (Kipp, 2001; Smith, 1990). A recent analysis of U.S. espionage cases by DoD's Personnel Security Research Center (PERSEREC) suggested that the threat posed by internal espionage, for a variety of reasons, has increased in recent years (Kramer, Heuer, & Crawford, 2005). This threat presents both a risk and an opportunity to CI efforts. Operations may be conducted to identify a suspected *mole* or insider providing information to hostile parties but may conversely involve the use of an insider to provide false leads and information to those parties. Psychologists can and do support both types of operations.

In counterespionage operations, assessing motivations is essential. According to a 2002 PERSEREC study of 150 espionage cases directed against the United States by U.S. citizens, insiders who betray their country's secrets rarely seek or enter their security position with intent to do so (Herbig & Wiskoff, 2002). This is true both for civilian and military cases. The idea or intent to engage in espionage usually comes to insiders some time after they are in their official position. Those in intelligence and communications-related positions are particularly well-represented, comprising approximately one third of all cases.

That internal spies are developed only after they are cleared and hired has some significant implications for both offensive and defensive counterespionage operations. It suggests the central importance of understanding vulnerabilities to seeking or being recruited by an FIS or other hostile entity (Crawford & Bosshardt, 1993). It also suggests that there are typically approach and avoidance motivational forces that operate to varying degrees in the individual's decision making. Motivations in espionage cases are typically multiple and often complex, frequently rife with ambivalence and competing needs and incentives. PERSEREC's research suggests that over the past 70 years the motivational profile of those committing treason may have changed from a dominant focus on ideology to a dominant focus on money (Thompson, 2001).

Shaw, Ruby, and Post (1998), for example, applied some of the findings from another government-sponsored study of insider spies, an unpublished research project entitled, "Project Slammer," to portray a "pathway" to espionage. They did not conduct the Slammer study but interpreted its findings. Their proposed pathway is composed of the following events: (a) predisposing personal traits, (b) an acute situational stressor, (c) emotional fallout, (d) biased decision making or judgment failures, and (e) failure of peers and supervisors to intervene effectively (Shaw et al., 1998).

The basic idea here is that there are often discernible precipitating events that produce observable changes in behavior before and during the period of actual betrayal. This is consistent with findings from the PERSEREC study in which one quarter of betrayers were known to have had a major life crisis in the months before turning to espionage, and 80% were known to have demonstrated one or more conditions or behaviors of security concern (Herbig & Wiskoff, 2002). Knowing the nature and frequency with which suitability concerns emerge in cases of insider betrayal before the espionage occurs can help to identify persons who may warrant greater interest in an investigation. The following case study offers an example of how operational psychology may play a salient role in counterespionage operations.

Case Study: Consultation in a Counterespionage Operation

A U.S. intelligence agency learned through credible, reliable sources that an FIS was receiving information from a Pentagon insider with access to sensitive information. Though the insider's identity was still unknown, certain demographic and travel-related information about him was discernible and allowed investigators to narrow the list of likely suspects from 2,300 to about 175. Doing a full investigation on all of them would be time- and labor intensive and could even alert the insider to the agency's suspicions. Needing a way to further narrow the list, investigators consulted an operational psychologist. The psychologist suggested to investigators that they might consider a strategy in which interviews are conducted under the cover of a government personnel study of security practices. He also advised them on certain strategies used in psychological research on deception that might help them to further parse the pool of interviewees into three categories of likely deception (i.e., high, moderate, and low). Using this method consistently across the interviews, the answers of only one respondent were markedly distinct from all others. This, of course, was not dispositive of that person's guilt, but he did continue to be of significant investigative interest, and months later, with substantial evidence collected, that individual was arrested for espionage. The psychological consultation was not for profiling or pinpointing the insider but to advise and offer suggestions to investigators based on knowledge of human behavior and psychological research that might help them rationally and systematically focus their investigative leads (Shumate & Borum, 2006).

Psychologists are also consultants to CT efforts. There is general consensus in the intelligence, defense, and diplomatic communities that transnational terrorism currently poses one of the most serious threats to U.S. national security. CI activities are a vital part of the overall U.S. strategy to combat terrorism, and DoD is at the heart of those efforts, including, but not limited to, force protection (Graham, 2002). Since 9/11 and throughout the Global War on Terrorism, U.S. military, intelligence, and law enforcement forces have had to reorient and redeploy resources to combat a nonstate adversary whose structure and operations are different from those of their past opponents and are constantly evolving (Borum, 2004; Borum & Gelles, 2005). Plainly, this requires a different type of operation and a different strategy (Wettering, 2000). The most aggressive and proactive of these operations typically require recruiting or inserting a source inside an operational terrorist cell. CI-driven source operations against terrorist targets can prevent specific attacks, interrupt forward motion, and sometimes yield valuable information. It is difficult, however, to access and infiltrate a security-conscious collective. To do so requires an understanding of behavior, interpersonal relationships, interpersonal influence, and group dynamics (Gelles, Borum, & Palarea, 2005). These conditions offer ample opportunity for psychological input. The following case study offers an example of how operational psychology may play a role in counterterrorism operations.

Case Study: Consultation in a Counterterrorism Operation

While investigating the recruitment activity of a local cluster (cell) of extremists suspected of planning a terrorist attack, a DoD official discovered that one of the extremists had a very long-standing relationship with a member of the U.S. Armed Forces, though the official suspected the service member was unaware of his friend's subversive connections and activity. Investigators knew that if the service member was amenable and effective, the relationship might provide an opportunity to collect vital information about terrorist activity. Because the two had been friends since childhood, however, the investigators also knew that recruiting the service member was potentially precarious. The investigative team sought consultation from an operational psychologist to assist with the following tasks: assessing the service member's suitability for such a task, providing behavioral information about him that would assist case officers in his management, and supporting the case handlers' ability to monitor dynamics throughout the operation. The psychologist suggested the team might consider a *trial run*, allowing the serviceman to act as a covert source in another smaller operation involving no people previously known to him. It was thought this might permit a more concrete assessment of the nature and degree of the serviceman's cooperation as well as his ability to follow tradecraft protocol and handle the stress and uncertainty of a covert role while also building mutual trust and confidence between the serviceman and case handlers. The service member performed well in the trial operation and subsequently passed a formal psychological assessment. The operational psychologist met again with case officers to discuss how best to present the information to the serviceman about his friend and to request his cooperation. When case officers did approach the service member, he related his own concerns about some of his old friend's changing attitudes and associations and expressed a willingness to help with the investigation in a covert role. During the course of the operation, the operational psychologist met twice with the service member to monitor his coping and psychological status and prepared a plan to help the service member debrief and psychologically readjust after the operation concluded (Shumate & Borum, 2006).

Psychological consultations in operational contexts can raise ethical concerns and even dilemmas that the 2002 APA Ethics Code did not foresee and was not designed to address. This does not necessarily mean, however, that the Ethics Code should not apply to these activities or even that it is insufficient to cover them. Both of those points remain as open questions. If psychologists are going to continue to provide services of benefit to national security and the specialty of operational psychology is to continue to evolve, then discussion of ethical issues, dilemmas, and principles must be earnest, thorough, and ongoing. In the following sections, we offer some initial ideas and pose some possible questions to contribute to this growing conversation.

COMMON ETHICAL DILEMMAS

A number of operationally trained psychologists working in the DoD CI community are developing processes and initiatives designed to help psychologists thoughtfully navigate ethical issues. For the past 5 years, psychology in-service sessions on ethics have been conducted in which CI psychologists present and discuss ethical questions and concerns. These sessions involve a number of senior psychologists who have security clearances and who may serve as consultants to other psychologists on ethical questions. What follows is a discussion of the problems regularly addressed in these ethics forums.

For certain ethical issues, such as involvement in torture, the applicability of the APA Ethics Code is unequivocally clear (APA, 2006, 2007, 2009; APA,

Presidential Task Force on Psychological Ethics and National Security, 2005; see Appendix). Its applicability or guidance on other issues, however, is more complex. One must resist the temptation to conclude that ethical issues as they relate to standards of practice are resolved or settled simply because one was addressing them in a particular way in the past. Ethical principles reflectively derived should guide psychologists' professional conduct. Psychologists should not, however, allow the fact that conduct has occurred in the past to drive a decision about whether it is ethically appropriate for the future. It is in this diffident and constructive spirit that we seek to contribute our thoughts and ideas.

In the "Ethical Principles of Psychologists and Code of Conduct" (APA, 2010), there is an effort to give guidance to psychologists on how to resolve ethical issues. The APA Ethics Code is particularly useful to operational psychologists facing difficult ethical challenges. Psychologists are encouraged to consult with their colleagues to help resolve ethical and professional dilemmas. Those psychologists serving in management positions are working to help effect policy changes that will mitigate many of the more vexing situations. One major example of this effort by some psychologists is to provide illustrative examples to the APA Ethics Committee as it writes a casebook and commentary on ethics and interrogations (APA, 2007).

APPLICATION OF THE APA ETHICS CODE TO COUNTERINTELLIGENCE AND COUNTERTERRORISM CONSULTATION

What follows is a discussion of selected portions of the Ethics Code that inform the operational psychologist consulting to CI and CT efforts. These identified aspects of the Ethics Code are considered the most pertinent, but by no means are they meant to be exhaustive.

Ethical Standard 1.01, Misuse of Psychologists' Work

"If psychologists learn of misuse or misrepresentation of their work, they take reasonable steps to correct or minimize the misuse or misrepresentation" (APA, 2010). The potential for misuse of operational psychologists' work certainly exists in CI and CT consultations. Such misuse happens rarely, but when it does, the psychologist is likely to become aware of it and be in a position to correct or minimize it. Usually, this entails correcting the misinterpretation(s) made by well-meaning operational personnel who may *read in* too much as they listen to and/or read the psychologist's oral and/or written report of psychological assessment or consultation. Therefore, when these situations arise it is important for psychologists to ensure their reports facilitate an accurate representation of their intended use and facilitate the services intended within the organization (see, e.g., Ethical Standards 6.01 and 4.01). When necessary, the psychologist should meet with operational personnel to ensure they understand the purpose and limitations of the report or assessment. Psychologists sometimes find it helpful to follow up or ask for a summary of what the reader thought and to remain cognizant of and clarify any potential misunderstandings. These situations are usually averted most easily when psychologists provide preliminary verbal feedback prior to writing the formal report. In these feedback sessions, the issues to be clarified in the report become clearer to the psychologist.

Ethical Standard 1.03, Conflicts Between Ethics and Organizational Demands

> If the demands of an organization with which psychologists are affiliated or for whom they are working conflict with this Ethics Code, psychologists clarify the nature of the conflict, make known their commitment to the Ethics Code, and to the extent feasible, resolve the conflict in a way that permits adherence to the Ethics Code. (APA, 2010)

In operational and investigative contexts, the potential often exists for conflicts between psychological ethics and the particular demands of the case. When ethical concerns arise, psychologists typically find allies in other psychologists and often in legal professionals who can help clarify for operational personnel the ethical and legal parameters of psychologists' participation. An example of conflict between organizational and ethical demands is illustrated in the case of a psychologist who performed psychological assessments at a foreign military base overseas. The ranking officer at the foreign base demanded to take possession of the psychologist's testing materials possibly to refute the psychologist's findings with which he did not agree. Although U.S. operational personnel pressured the psychologist to comply, she asserted herself to protect the integrity of the psychological test materials. After much discussion, the psychologist convinced the commander that he did not need to take possession of the tests. She explained to him the types of questions being asked, why these questions were being asked, how they were being used in the assessment process as well as her professional duty and commitment to protect the integrity of the test items. After the explanation, the ranking officer withdrew his request/demand.

Ethical Standard 2.01, Boundaries of Competence

> (a) Psychologists provide services, teach, and conduct research with populations and in areas only within the boundaries of their competence,

based on their education, training, supervised experience, consultation, study, or professional experience.

(e) In those emerging areas in which generally recognized standards for preparatory training do not yet exist, psychologists nevertheless take reasonable steps to ensure the competence of their work and to protect clients/patients, students, supervisees, research participants, organizational clients, and others from harm. (APA, 2010)

What are the boundaries of competence for psychologists consulting to CI and CT operations and investigations? Given the lack of established standards, psychologists in the operational arena grapple with this question. In the post-9/11 world, the field of operational psychology has been growing both in size and scope. But the field is still relatively young, with questions of how best to establish competence still being developed and explored (Stephenson & Staal, 2007b).

Despite the fact that this specialty area is only just evolving, training practices are rapidly emerging in response to the need. Psychologists working on CI issues within the DoD have implemented a wide variety of training practices to ensure role-specific competency. As an initial effort, operational psychologists working for DoD have engaged their colleagues in the operational arena on an informal basis to share knowledge. In addition, in 2004, the DoD CI behavioral science program received APA's approval to offer continuing education (CE) for psychologists. As a result, for the past 5 years, CE programs have been offered regularly for operational psychologists. These training opportunities are designed to increase competence and educate newly initiated psychologists in understanding and navigating the differences between applying psychological science and methods in an operational venue as opposed to a clinical and/or forensic practice setting. As such, a focused discussion of ethical dilemmas is a routine part of these CE programs. Stephenson and Staal (2007a) recommended the use of a "naturalistic decision model that integrates rational and intuitive elements" (p. 61) to assist psychologists in resolving ethical dilemmas in operational settings. In this approach, operational psychologists are encouraged to ask questions regarding the safety, legality, ethicality, and effectiveness of their activities with an emphasis on principles of fidelity, responsibility, integrity, and respect for others' rights and dignity. In the CE programs, the use of this model has proven useful in systematically considering the merits as well as the potential hazards posed by different courses of action.

Ethical Standard 3.07, Third-Party Requests for Services

When psychologists agree to provide services to a person or entity at the request of a third party, psychologists attempt to clarify at the outset of the service the nature of the relationship with all individuals or organizations involved. This clarification includes the role of the psychologist (e.g., therapist, consultant, diagnostician, or expert witness), an identification of who is the client, the probable uses of the services provided or the information obtained, and the fact that there may be limits to confidentiality. (p. 1065)

Professional dilemmas involving psychologists' roles and responsibilities in CI and CT activities often center on the question "Who is the client?" It is generally agreed that the U.S. government (USG) is the operational psychologist's primary client. The USG is the organizational entity that requests, receives, and acts on the information psychologists provide. Ethical psychologists also recognize, however, that even in operational settings, psychologists have a dual responsibility to consider the impact on the person being evaluated, even if he or she is not "the" client. Accordingly, when possible, operational psychologists obtain informed consent for formal psychological assessments (see APA Ethical Standards 3.10 and 9.03) to ensure that the purpose of the evaluation and the limits of confidentiality are clearly explained and to clarify for the examinee whether he or she will receive feedback on the results of the psychological assessment (see APA Ethical Standard 9.10). Often it is impractical or impossible to provide complete feedback. For example, in situations in which either the person being evaluated or the psychologist is flying in from a distant land and time in country is extremely limited, usually only preliminary feedback is possible. In the examples provided previously, the issue of balancing the interests of the USG with those of the person being assessed is critical. In the first case, an unknown subject, a malicious insider, was detected by USG investigators with assistance from a psychologist. The psychologist in this case never met with the individual because it was not appropriate to do so. In the second case, a service member was evaluated face-to-face by a psychologist. Informed consent was obtained, and the person willingly participated in the evaluation process. The recommendations that followed from the psychologist adequately addressed the operational concerns of the USG while ethically weighing the safety aspects and the effectiveness of the service member's involvement in the operational activity. This led to an experiment to evaluate how well the service member would deal with the stresses of operational activity. Ultimately, the case was successful when the proper safeguards were put in place by the case officer with the assistance of the psychologist.

Additionally, operational psychologists must make known the limitations of the assessment and conclusions (APA Ethical Standard 9.10). In a minority of cases, a psychologist is asked to render an opinion on an operational matter regarding a particular individual when it is not operationally appropriate or possible for the psychologist to interview and acquire test results from that individual. Most psychologists view this as a preliminary consultation in which they draw on their knowledge of human psychology, foreign cultures, and operations to develop hypotheses and suggestions for how one might approach and interact with a particular individual or group. Because the information provided to psychologists in these situations is often incomplete, the consulting operational psychologist clarifies the limitations of his or her opinions and how these limitations might impact the reliability and usefulness of the conclusions reached. The psychologist also suggests what information would be required to help form a more robust opinion (see APA Ethical Standard 9.01) and methods for collecting that information in an effective and ethically appropriate manner. Moreover, Morgan et al. (2006) suggested that operational consultants performing these types of preliminary consultations keep in mind three key ethical issues: adhering to sound professional judgment, recognizing the limits of their expertise, and identifying the client (e.g., law enforcement, DoD).

Ethical Standard 9.01, Bases for Assessments

"Psychologists base the opinions contained in their recommendations, reports, and diagnostic or evaluative statements, including forensic testimony, on information and techniques sufficient to substantiate their findings" (APA, 2010). Which assessment methods are appropriate for which kinds of operational and national security situations? Although some clinical and forensic psychological assessment methods have direct applicability in the operational arena, many do not. Operational and national security psychologists face certain challenges when reaching conclusions and making recommendations on the basis of traditional psychological measures. Operational psychologists make every attempt to adhere to the principles that deal with assessment issues as contained in Section 9, Assessment, of the APA Ethics Code. Potential dilemmas include the following:

- Reasons for assessment and the use of assessment results are often different in the operational arena than in clinical and forensic practice. For example, in the operational arena, the primary concern of those requesting consultation rarely involves the diagnosis of a mental or emotional condition. What is usually needed is a thorough analysis of a person's strengths, limitations, motivations, beliefs, attitudes, values, and more and how each may affect the mission. This requires that the psychologist understand operational dynamics, goals, and processes as well as the impact of foreign cultures on human behavior.
- When psychological testing is appropriate, questions of language, culture, and applicability must often be considered. For example, is construct validity maintained in both translation

from the original language to the foreign language and the *back translation* from the foreign language to the original language? Are there relevant norms for the particular population to which the individual belongs? Is the purpose for which the test is being used consistent with the purpose for which the test was developed?

- Psychologists using most commercially available assessment instruments are frequently in a position of needing to clarify the strengths and limitations of test results and their interpretation (per APA Ethical Standards 9.02 and 9.06).

- In some cases, psychologists have attempted to develop new tools or techniques to facilitate the assessment process in the operational arena. However, given constraints on monetary and human resources as well as time, it can be difficult to develop these tools in such a way that they are useful as well as valid and reliable (see APA Ethical Standard 9.05).

CONCLUSION

Potential misuse of a psychologist's work, conflict between ethics and organizational demands, competence, privacy and confidentiality, and assessment are key areas in which psychologists working in national security environments face challenges. In all cases, we encourage psychologists providing consultation services in the operational arena to consider some of the following questions as they do their work:

1. Who is my client? If the client is the USG and the operational activity involves psychological assessment of an individual, what professional ethical obligations do I have toward the person being assessed?
2. Have I taken the opportunity to discuss my findings with the client before committing my thoughts to writing?
3. Have I been clear with myself and my client regarding the limitations of the methods I am using?
4. Have I carefully considered the safety, legality, ethicality, and effectiveness of my methods before I proceed?
5. (If new to the area of operational applications of psychology) Have I sought adequate training and supervision in the arena of operational consultation?
6. (When faced with an ethical dilemma) Have I sought input from my peers in operational psychology prior to pursuing a particular course of action?

The authors are currently working through appropriate DoD channels to effect policy changes designed to address some of these challenges. In addition, for the past 5 years, the DoD CI Behavioral Science community has initiated a broad range of thoughtful and systematic research into areas of ethical and effective elicitation and interviewing methods, cross-cultural communications, source assessment tools, and other issues of relevance to the DoD CI community. Until professional standards of practice and a tailored code of ethics are agreed upon in the arena of operational psychology, it is the shared belief of the authors that by consulting with colleagues and thoroughly considering particular cases and situations, psychologists can and will find solutions to complex questions that permit both continued adherence to the APA Ethics Code and effective consultation to CI and CT operations in service of national security.

REFERENCES

American Psychological Association. (2006). *Resolution against torture and other cruel, inhuman, and degrading treatment or punishment*. Retrieved April 23, 2008, from http://www.apa.org/governance/resolutions/notortureres.html

American Psychological Association (2007). *Reaffirmation of the American Psychological Association position against torture and other cruel, inhuman, or degrading treatment or punishment and its application to individuals defined in the United States Code as "enemy combatants."* Retrieved April 23, 2008, from http://www.apa.org/governance/resolutions/councilres0807.html

American Psychological Association. (2009). Psychologists and Unlawful Detention Settings With a Focus on National Security. Washington, DC: Author. Retrieved on January 15, 2010, from http://www.apa.org/about/governance/council/policy/chapter-4b.aspx#unlawful-detention

American Psychological Association. (2010). *Ethical principles of psychologists and code of conduct (2002, Amended June 1, 2010)*. Retrieved from http://www.apa.org/ethics/code/index.aspx

American Psychological Association, Presidential Task Force on Psychological Ethics and National Security. (2005, June). *Report of the American Psychological Association Presidential Task Force on Psychological Ethics and National Security*. Retrieved April 23, 2008, from http://www.apa.org/releases/PENSTaskForceReportFinal.pdf

Behnke, S. (2007, December). A call for vignettes. *Monitor on Psychology, 38*, 66–67.

Borum, R. (2004). *Psychology of terrorism*. Tampa: University of South Florida Press.

Borum, R., & Gelles, M. (2005). The operational and organizational evolution of Al-Qaeda: A behavioral perspective. *Behavioral Sciences & the Law, 23*, 467–483.

Borum, R., Super, J., & Rand, M. (2003). Forensic assessment for high-risk occupations. In A. Goldstein (Ed.), *Comprehensive handbook of psychology: Vol. 11. Forensic psychology* (pp. 133–148). New York: Wiley.

Crawford, K. S., & Bosshardt, M. J. (1993). *Assessment of position factors that increase vulnerability to espionage*. Monterey, CA: Defense Personnel Security Research Center.

Exec. Order No. 12,333, 46 F.R. 59941 (1981).

Gelles, M., Borum, R., & Palarea, R. (2005). *Fundamentals of jihadism: Behavioral considerations for developing and managing counterterrorism sources*. Washington, DC: Naval Criminal Investigative Service.

Graham, J. (2002). *What the U.S. military can do to defeat terrorism*. Lincoln, NE: Writer's Club Press.

Herbig, K. L. & Wiskoff, M. F. (2002). *Espionage against the United States by American citizens: 1947–2001*. Monterey, CA: Defense Personnel Security Research Center.

Kipp, S. (2001). *Espionage and the insider*. San Francisco: SANS Institute.

Kramer, L., Heuer, R., & Crawford, K. (2005). *Technological, social, and economic trends that are increasing U.S. vulnerability to insider espionage*. Monterey, CA: Defense Personnel Security Research Center.

Morgan, C. A., Gelles, M. G., Steffian, G., Coric, V., Temporini, H., Fortunati, F., et al. (2006). Consulting to government agencies—indirect assessments. *Psychiatry, 3,* 2–6.

National Security Agency. (2001). *Espionage: The threat is real*. Washington, DC: Author.

Olson, J. (2001). The ten commandments of counterintelligence. *Studies on Intelligence, 11,* 81–87.

Shaw, E. D., Ruby, K. G., & Post, J. M. (1998). *The insider threat to information systems* (Security Awareness Bulletin No. 2-98). Washington, DC: U.S. Department of Defense Security Institute.

Shumate, R. S., & Borum, R. (2006). Psychological consultation in defense counterintelligence operations. *Military Psychology, 18,* 283–296.

Smith, E. (1990). The spies among us: Trends in military espionage. *American Intelligence Journal, 11,* 1–3.

Stephenson, J. A., & Staal, M. A. (2007a). An ethical decision-making model for operational psychology. *Ethics &Behavior, 17,* 61–82.

Stephenson, J. A., & Staal, M. A. (2007b). Operational psychology: What constitutes expertise? *The ABPP Specialist, 13,* 30–31.

Thompson, T. (2001). Security and motivational factors in espionage. *American Intelligence Journal, 20,* 47–56.

Wettering, F. (2000). Counterintelligence: The broken triad. *International Journal of Intelligence and Counterintelligence, 13,* 265–300.

5

BEHAVIORAL SCIENCE CONSULTATION TO INTERROGATION AND DEBRIEFING OPERATIONS: ETHICAL CONSIDERATIONS

DEBRA DUNIVIN, L. MORGAN BANKS, MARK A. STAAL, AND JAMES A. STEPHENSON

The use of psychologists to provide operational support to the military is not new. Much of applied psychology started with support of military operations in World War I and World War II (e.g., Britt & Morgan, 1946; Layman, 1943; McGuire, 1990; Melton, 1957). However, application of psychological expertise to support military commanders to attain strategic goals in a theater of war and facilitate intelligence operations requires a significant paradigm shift for many psychologists (Shumate & Borum, 2006; Williams, Picano, Roland, & Banks, 2006). Professional ethics is a central issue.

Behavioral science consultation, as described in this chapter, is an area of practice that applies psychological science to interrogation and debriefing operations. Psychologists and other experts in behavioral science have consulted to law enforcement and intelligence agencies in both civilian and military settings for many years. The Federal Bureau of Investigation and Naval Criminal Investigative Service, for example, use these subject matter experts both as individuals and in teams or behavioral science units.

The opinions contained in this chapter are the views of the authors and do not represent official policy or positions of the U.S. Department of Defense, U.S. Department of the Army, or U.S. Department of the Air Force.

Some operational definitions may be helpful. A working definition of interrogation is the "questioning related to law enforcement or to military and national security intelligence gathering, designed to prevent harm or danger to individuals, the public, or national security" (American Medical Association Council on Ethical and Judicial Affairs, 2006, p. 212). Debriefing is another form of questioning used in law enforcement or intelligence activities. However, a distinction is that individuals being interrogated are usually in the custody of those conducting the questioning, whereas individuals being debriefed are usually not in custody (U. S. Department of the Army Headquarters [DA HQ], 2006). A useful working definition of a behavioral science consultant is a psychologist or other "health care personnel qualified in behavioral sciences who [is] assigned exclusively to provide consultative services to support authorized law enforcement or intelligence activities" (U.S. Department of Defense [DoD], 2006b, p. 2). It is very important to note that behavioral science consultants are "not assigned to clinical practice functions, but to provide consultative services to . . . activities including detention and related intelligence, interrogation, and detainee debriefing operations" (U.S. Department of the Army Office of the Surgeon General [DA OTSG], 2010, p. 4).

The crux of the ethical dilemma surrounding consultation to interrogation and other national security activities lies within the weighing of competing positive values, a process often required when making decisions about one's behavior as a professional. Analyses of the ethical dilemmas that emerge when psychologists apply their expertise in the interest of national security are not new (see, e.g., Grisso, 2001). The need to analyze ethical dilemmas in the provision of psychological services within social organizations or systems is also not new. For example, an American Psychological Association (APA) task force from 1975 through 1978 examined in depth the ways in which psychologists interact in and with the criminal justice system and the ethical issues such interactions create (Monahan, 1980).

In this chapter, we address some of these issues and describe the legal parameters and ethical standards that exist for psychologists providing behavioral science consultation to interrogation and debriefing operations. Relevant Geneva Convention protocols, federal policy guidelines (including congressional), and DoD policies are reviewed. In this chapter, we build on the literature already available in the law enforcement arena, including the practices of police psychologists, and present several potential ethical dilemmas that might arise when supporting these types of activities. The scenarios are discussed in the context of legal parameters, doctrinal and policy guidance, and the APA (2010) "Ethical Principles of Psychologists and Code of Conduct."

THE CRUX OF THE ETHICAL DILEMMA

Central to the ethical analysis of psychologists' consultation to military interrogations and other national security operations is the balance that must be established between ethical responsibilities to an individual and ethical responsibilities to the larger society. Principle A, Beneficence and Nonmaleficence, or "do no harm," of the APA Ethics Code (APA, 2010) establishes that psychologists have ethical responsibilities to the individuals being questioned. Principle B, Fidelity and Responsibility, establishes that psychologists have ethical responsibilities to other individuals and to the general public. As Behnke (2006) so concisely stated, "by virtue of Principle A psychologists do no harm; by virtue of Principle B psychologists use their expertise in, and understanding of, human behavior to aid in the prevention of harm" (p. 66).

The profession of psychology is extremely broad, with psychologists working in diverse fields. Some psychologists are mental health professionals who provide clinical services to patients, but many are not. Some psychologists are employed by companies or by the U.S. government to assist in screening individuals to help ensure suitability for employment in general or for specific duties (e.g., Picano, Roland, Rollins, & Williams, 2002; see also chap. 2, this volume). Other psychologists work providing consulting advice to advertising agencies supporting a myriad of commercial products. In forensic settings, psychologists provide objective evaluations of individuals involved in legal disputes. Psychologists in the employ of law enforcement provide support to the screening process of police officers, to the crisis negotiation process (see chap. 6, this volume), and to the legal questioning of criminal suspects. In addition, these police psychologists assist in the apprehension and conviction of criminals by developing behavioral profiles. In some of these cases, the decision making and assessments made by the psychologist may facilitate a negative outcome for a specific individual in the interests of protecting society. In no case is that more apparent than when a police psychologist provides consultation that assists in the arrest and conviction of a criminal; this is especially true when the result may be the death penalty. Criminal justice examples were explored in depth by Monahan (1980).

In most of these settings, the client is not an individual but instead is an organization. Nevertheless, regardless of the setting, psychologists have an ethical responsibility to both the individuals with whom they work and to society as well as to the organizations within which they work. As an example of this mixed agency, a clinician treating children is required to maintain confidentiality but may need to break that trust under certain specific circumstances, such as child abuse reporting. This may result in the criminal prosecution of other individuals (e.g., a parent, caretaker). The ethical assessment revolves around relative harm to the various parties. In other words, does the protection of the child outweigh breeching confidentiality of the exchange with the child and, potentially, the privacy of other parties?

In the military setting, there are unique elements of psychological practice that may amplify ethical quandaries such as balancing interests of the individual with those of the larger organization (e.g., Johnson, 1995; 2008; Staal & King, 2000). In his discussion of ethical challenges for military clinical psychologists, Johnson (2008) maintained that "there may be times when a psychologist encounters clear incongruence between the best interests of a client and the best interest of the larger military or the immediate mission" (p. 53). He described the ethically challenging conflict that would emerge when a military objective might depend on returning to duty a service member who has a psychological impairment.

Struggling with the ethical dilemma of balancing obligations to individuals and to society when supporting national security activities, as previously noted, is not new. Take, for example, Grisso's (2001) ethical analysis of a psychologist who assisted the Federal Bureau of Investigation, for whom he worked, in devising a plan to catch an alleged spy, Theresa Squillacote. The plan played on Ms. Squillacote's emotional vulnerability and lured her into a situation that resulted in her capture. Grisso considered the notion that psychologists can never do "harm" (in any degree) as overly simplistic and cited a number of situations in which individuals might be harmed by actions required of psychologists in the usual course of clinical work. All of these situations were within legal boundaries of the roles given psychologists by society and involved weighing potential harm to the individual against social consequences of failing to address the possibility of harm that a given individual might commit against another. Grisso acknowledged that "how a professional weighs the competing positive values in cases such as this depends in part on the professional's own values" (p. 459) and concluded that "in principle, the mere fact that the psychologist placed considerable weight on society's interests and acted in a way that would harm the individual in question does not violate the APA's code of ethics" (p. 460). Despite not being new, this ethical analysis lies within the core of the debate regarding psychologists' participation in interrogation and detainee operations.

Following the September 11, 2001, terrorist attacks on the United States, the U.S. military began to detain individuals believed to be involved in or knowledgeable about terrorism activities. The U.S. military had not conducted large-scale in-depth intelligence interrogations since the Korean War. As the DoD began to conduct interrogations, some military psychologists began to provide consultation in support of questioning these detainees in a manner very similar to that of police psychologists. As this support developed, the value of having a psychologist involved became apparent, especially given psychologists' understanding of such issues as the prevention of behavioral drift and moral disengagement.

The concept of behavioral drift may be defined as "the continual re-establishment of new, often unstated, and unofficial standards in an unintended direction" (DA OTSG, 2010, p. 5). It may also be defined as a gradual, progressive "deviation from professionally and ethically acceptable behavior [something that] psychologists, as experts in human behavior, are trained to observe and intervene to prevent" when observing interrogations (Behnke, 2006, p. 67). Behavioral drift is a particular concern in guards and interrogators and may arise in situations in which there are "ambiguous guidance, poor supervision, and lack of training and oversight" (DA OTSG, 2010, p. 5). This phenomenon may be observed in settings where individuals have power over significant aspects of other's lives and can be seen in Zimbardo's famous prison experiments (Haney, Banks, & Zimbardo, 1973; Zimbardo, 1971). Signs of behavioral drift must be monitored frequently to prevent any harm to individuals and detriment to the mission.

Moral disengagement, a set of cognitive mechanisms that diminish moral self-regulatory processes (Bandura, 1986), is a phenomenon that often accompanies behavioral drift. Recent research in this area explores individual differences correlated with moral disengagement (Detert, Trevino, & Sweitzer, 2008). These mechanisms are believed to serve as the psychological under-pinnings that occur with the disengagement of regulatory self-sanctions, allowing potentially harmful acts to become linked to worthy purposes (Bandura, Barbaranelli, Caprara, & Pastorelli, 1996), thereby creating the relationship between disengagement of moral self-sanctions and support of military force and lethal means (McAlister, Bandura, & Owen, 2006).

RELEVANT LAW

The conduct of armed hostilities on land is regulated by *The Law of Land Warfare* articulated in the *Army Field Manual* (FM 27-10; U.S. Department of Army [DA], 1956). The purpose of such law is to protect combatants and noncombatants from unnecessary suffering, to safeguard the fundamental human rights of persons who fall into the hands of the enemy, and to facilitate the restoration of peace. Included in this body of law are several treaties to which the United States is a signatory. Two of these, in particular, are directly relevant.

The Geneva Convention Relative to the Treatment of Prisoners of War of August 12, 1949, lays out how prisoners of war must be treated when captured. The Geneva Convention Relative to the Protection of Civilian Persons in Time of War of August 12, 1949, outlines the required treatment of civilians who are detained by military forces. A thorough discussion of the Geneva Conventions and the requirements for them to take effect is well beyond the scope of this chapter. Some discussion of the conventions, however, is essential to understanding the legal parameters of detention operations. Specifically, Article 3 is the article that is common to several Geneva Conventions, and it is often referred to as Common Article 3. Article 3 states that detainees "shall in all circumstances be treated humanely, without any adverse distinction founded on race, colour [sic], religion or faith, sex, birth or wealth, or any other similar criteria" (United Nations Office of the High Commissioner for Human Rights, 1949, p. 4). It goes on to prohibit the following acts:

> at any time and in any place whatsoever with respect to the above-mentioned persons: (a) violence to life and person, in particular murder of all kinds, mutilation, cruel treatment and torture; (b) taking of hostages; (c) outrages upon personal dignity, in particular, humiliating and degrading treatment. (p. 5)

Much of the controversy surrounding interrogation and other national security activities has centered on how torture is defined, what constitutes humiliating and degrading treatment, and what rights are afforded detained individuals. These issues will continue to be debated and discussed in the law, in literature, and in national and international forums. However, interrogation practice should draw on the U.S. Department of Justice Office of Legal Counsel (DOJ OLC) opinions interpreting the federal criminal prohibition against torture (DOJ OLC, 2002; superseded by DOJ OLC, 2004). These analyses cite many specific examples of what actions have and have not been defined as torture at the state, federal, and international levels and draw distinctions between torture and other forms of cruel, inhuman, and degrading treatment with their foundation in the Geneva Conventions. Drawing from the more recent text,

> Torture is abhorrent both to American law and values and to international norms. This universal repudiation of torture is reflected in our criminal law, for example, 18 U.S.C. §§ 2340-2340A; international agreements, exemplified by the United Nations Convention Against Torture (the "CAT")[1]; customary international law [2]; centuries of Anglo-American law[3]; and the longstanding policy of the United States, repeatedly and recently reaffirmed by the President. [4] (DOJ OLC, 2004, p. 1; footnote hyperlinks contained only in the original source)

Since the passage of the Detainee Treatment Act of 2005 (often referred to as the McCain amendment), it has been U.S. law to treat detainees in accordance with Common Article 3. This was codified by Deputy Secretary of Defense Gordon England's July 7, 2006, memo and the subsequent DoD directive, *The Department of Defense Detainee Program* (No. 2310.01E; DoD, 2006a), requiring that all detainees held by DoD be treated in accordance with Article 3.

DOCTRINAL GUIDANCE REGARDING INTERROGATION AND DEBRIEFING OPERATIONS

Interrogation and debriefing are two categories of human intelligence (HUMINT) collection; these activities vary depending on the source of information and methodology. Doctrinal guidance for these activities, that is, the authoritative body of thought on how U.S. Army leaders and soldiers should operate, is provided in *Human Intelligence Collector Operations* (FM 2-22.3; DA HQ, 2006). Interrogation is defined as "the systematic effort to procure information to answer specific collection requirements by direct and indirect questioning techniques of a person who is in the custody of the forces conducting the questioning" (DA HQ, 2006, para. 1-20). This is a more technical definition than the working definition provided earlier in this chapter. It is required that interrogations be conducted only by personnel who are appropriately trained and certified by the U.S. Army Intelligence Center or other defense HUMINT management office designated agency in accordance with guidance established by the Under Secretary of Defense (Intelligence). It is further required that they must always be conducted in accordance with U.S. law, including the Uniform Code of Military Justice, Geneva Conventions, and Detainee Treatment Act of 2005, regardless of the source's level of cooperation which could be expected to range from cooperative to antagonistic.

Debriefing is another HUMINT collection activity that is defined as "the process of questioning cooperating human sources to satisfy intelligence requirements, consistent with applicable law. The source [in a debriefing] usually is not in custody [of the forces conducting the questioning as is the subject of interrogation] and usually is willing to cooperate" (DA HQ, 2006, para. 1-21). The purpose of this questioning is to gather information that will prevent harm to individual persons, the general public, or national security, an obligation that must be weighed against individual rights.

Human Intelligence Collector Operations (FM 2-22.3; DA HQ, 2006) expressly endorses Geneva Conventions Common Article 3, the Detainee Treatment Act of 2005, and expressly prohibits torture and any other cruel, inhuman, or degrading treatment. The field manual identifies a multifaceted rationale for this prohibition in the context of interrogations and other intelligence collection activities:

> Use of torture is not only illegal but also it is a poor technique that yields unreliable results, may damage subsequent collection efforts, and can induce the source to say what he thinks the HUMINT collector wants to hear. Use of torture can also have many possible negative consequences at national and international levels. (DA HQ, 2006, para. 5-74)

Some of the specific prohibitions cited in this document are sexual humiliation, hooding, use of military working dogs, and waterboarding. *Human*

Intelligence Collector Operations (FM 2-22.3; DA HQ, 2006) further acknowledges that it may be difficult at times to distinguish between permissible and prohibited actions and outlines steps to be taken when there is any doubt that the techniques are in accordance with applicable law. These steps include stopping the interrogation immediately and consulting with the chain of command for additional guidance (DA HQ, 2006, paras. 5-75–5-77).

The interrogation approaches and techniques listed in *Human Intelligence Collector Operations* (FM 2-22.3; DA HQ, 2006) are the only ones authorized for use by U.S. military personnel in accordance with the Detainee Treatment Act of 2005. This document establishes, as did the previous version of the field manual (FM 34-52), that an interrogation plan must be written and approved prior to implementation and provides detailed methodology for conducting these intelligence collection operations. The field manual underscores the importance of cultural awareness and an understanding of basic human behavior to successfully elicit accurate information from an individual. Applied psychological concepts are relied on heavily in discussions of the importance of developing a relationship, building rapport, categories of questions (e.g., direct, indirect), and types of questions that are unproductive for eliciting accurate information (e.g., leading, compound, vague). As experts in behavior and human interactions, psychologists have considerable knowledge that could facilitate success in conducting these operations; *Human Intelligence Collector Operations* notes that behavioral science consultants might be an available resource for interrogators and debriefers but does not dictate parameters of their consultative activities and thus does not serve as a policy document. Psychologists who apply their expertise in the interests of national security, including the application of psychological expertise to interrogation operations, must engage and balance both their societal and professional obligations to ensure their activities remain within policy guidance and align with the relevant ethical and legal parameters for their profession.

POLICY GUIDANCE REGARDING BEHAVIORAL SCIENCE CONSULTATION

In addition to the laws and conventions discussed previously, there are a number of directives and instructions from the DoD that are relevant for detainee operations. These DoD directives and instructions prohibit acts of physical or mental torture and reaffirm the expectation that all captured or detained persons will be treated humanely and any violations will be promptly reported and investigated. They also specifically regulate the use of psychologists during interrogations. The DoD directive *DoD Intelligence Interrogations, Detainee Debriefings, and Tactical Questioning* (No. 3115.09; DoD, 2005) authorizes behavioral science consultants "to make psychological assessments of the character, personality, social interactions, and other behavioral characteristics of interrogation subjects, and to advise authorized personnel performing lawful interrogations regarding such assessments" (p. 3) while prohibiting provision of medical care except in an emergency.

The DoD instruction *Medical Program Support for Detainee Operations* (No. 2310.08; DoD, 2006b) was released in June 2006. This instruction provides more detailed guidance on personnel providing behavioral science consultation in support of law enforcement and intelligence activities. *Medical Program Support for Detainee Operations* defines behavioral science consultants and details the standards and procedures for their use. In particular, and in a manner very similar to the support offered by police psychologists, it allows the use of behavioral science consultants to make psychological assessments of detainees in order to advise authorized personnel performing lawful interrogations, those making determinations of release or continued detention, and those responsible for detainee operations and maintaining the detention facility environment. As noted previously, it prohibits those behavioral science consultants who are supporting interrogations from providing their consultation and/or support to interrogations not in accordance with applicable laws and from performing any medical care except under emergency circumstances.

In October 2006, the Army Medical Command (MEDCOM) released detailed policy guidance on the use of psychologists and psychiatrists supporting interrogation and detainee operations (DA OTSG, 2006) and updated that policy in 2009 (DA OTSG, 2010). Because the Army is the proponent for detainee operations, this document, *Behavioral Science Consultation Policy*, gives specific guidance to all DoD psychologists when working in this area. It specifically prohibits abusive treatment of detainees and goes into detail on what psychologists are allowed and not allowed to do while in this role, and underscores the requirement that psychologists providing support to interrogations may not provide any medical care to detainees except under emergency situations (something that would be extremely rare). The following is directly excerpted from the policy document:

a. The mission of a BSC [behavioral science consultant] is to provide psychological expertise and consultation in order to assist the command in conducting safe, legal, ethical, and effective detention operations, intelligence interrogations, and detainee debriefing operations.
b. This mission is composed of two complementary objectives:
(1) To provide psychological expertise in monitoring, consultation, and feedback regarding the whole of the detention environment in order to assist the command in ensuring the humane treatment of detainees, prevention of abuse, and safety of U.S. personnel.

(2) To provide psychological expertise to assess the individual detainee and his environment and provide recommendations to improve the effectiveness of intelligence interrogations and detainee debriefing operations. (DA OTSG, 2010, p. 6)

As this policy guidance makes clear, the mission of psychologists supporting intelligence interrogations and detainee debriefings requires that psychologists ensure the interrogations and debriefings are conducted safely. Only then are the psychologists able to improve the effectiveness of the interrogation process. Even the order of the words in the mission statement, "safe, legal, ethical, and effective," requires the psychologists to first ensure safety, then legality. If those two requirements are met, then the psychologist must follow the extant ethical guidelines. (Notably, the APA Ethics Code [APA, 2010] has been incorporated into psychologist license requirements in more than half the states in the country.) Only then, once these three requirements are met, safe, legal, and ethical, may the behavioral science consultant focus on helping make the interrogation or debriefing more effective.

In addition to providing detailed guidance on the mission and objectives of behavioral science consultation, the MEDCOM policy (DA OTSG, 2006, 2010) details what behavioral science personnel may and may not do when serving in this capacity. The policy guidance delineates various tasks including assessment and consultation of interrogations and debriefings, indirect assessment, and consultation on the environmental setting. This document also establishes training requirements and prerequisites for psychologists and psychiatrists who undertake these assignments. Required training for personnel serving on behavioral science consultation teams (BSCTs) includes relevant law and doctrine on interrogation and detention operations; ethical guidance provided by professional associations; pertinent areas of behavioral science; cultural, religious, and ideological issues regarding the populations under consideration; dynamics of captivity; and risk management and oversight in detention settings (see, e.g., Fein, Lehner, & Vossekuil, 2006; Shumate, Borum, Turner, & Fogarty, 2006; and also Borum, Gelles, & Kleinman, 2009; Rahe & Geneder, 1983; Hannah, Clutterbuck, & Rubin, 2008 for discussions of some of these topics).

A third of this MEDCOM policy document on behavioral science consultation is devoted to a discussion of professional ethics. Included as attachments to the policy are reports from the American Psychological Association Presidential Task Force on Psychological Ethics and National Security (APA PENS, 2005; see Appendix) and the American Medical Association's Council on Ethical and Judicial Affairs (2006), a position statement of the American Psychiatric Association (2006), and ethical guidelines of the American Academy of Psychiatry and the Law (2005).

ETHICAL CONSIDERATIONS AND POTENTIAL DILEMMAS

The following scenarios delineate potential ethical dilemmas that may arise when providing behavioral science consultation to interrogation and debriefing operations. The scenarios illustrate application of a competency-based ethical and legal decision-making model as psychologists attempt to resolve these complex hypothetical situations. This model serves as a viable foundation when practicing in relatively new operational areas (Staal & Stephenson, 2006; Stephenson & Staal, 2007a; Williams et al., 2006). Psychologists providing behavioral science consultation to interrogation and debriefing operations

> will often have to use their professional judgment to assess situations and make decisions about what to do or not to do; maintain self-awareness of their role and responsibilities by using self-reflective practices to modify their decisions as appropriate; and carry out their actions in accord with the ethical principles, standards, guidelines, and values of the profession, with the understanding that competency is context-dependent, with the execution of that competency varying with the setting and environment. (Williams et al., 2006, p. 206)

Included with each scenario is a discussion of the different perspectives or sources of rules and components of the APA Ethics Code that might govern the psychologist's conduct and decision-making process in that situation.

Scenario 1: Mixing Behavioral Health Support With Interrogation Support

A psychologist assigned as part of a BSCT was working in a theater detention facility in Iraq. The facility had recently in-processed a suspected terrorist who was believed by military intelligence to possess information about terrorist planning and/or locations. Specifically, this subject was believed to have critical information associated with a pending large-scale attack against the facility, and he acknowledged as much during his initial screening. Moreover, he was found with a number of incriminating items to include bomb-making devices, instructional manuals, and explosives equipment. However, after his initial interrogation he stopped talking and began to act "crazy." The BSCT psychologist observed his interactions and read the interrogation reports describing this unusual behavior. From these sources of information it appeared obvious to the psychologist that the observed behavior and reported history of the suspected terrorist were inconsistent with a genuine mental health disorder or stress reaction and, instead, appeared to reflect a case of malingering. Aware of the fact that the BSCT psychologist was an expert in behavior and mental health and knowing that he had been able to observe the evolution of the detainee's behavior, the lead interrogator requested that he evaluate the detainee's mental status to provide guidance to the interrogation team on how to proceed.

In this instance, the dilemma was clear. In many ways it would be quite natural for the psychologist in this scenario to provide the requested assessment in order to facilitate the safe and effective interrogation of the detainee, weeding through a determination of whether his behavior was genuine or contrived. However, in doing so, the psychologist would enter into a multiple role relationship with the detainee and the interrogation team. Moreover, such a decision begs the question, Is it appropriate to mix such duties as a consultant to the interrogation team with those of health care provider to the detainee? Fortunately, the guidance for this case is relatively clear. According to Standard 3.05, Multiple Relationships, of the Ethics Code (APA, 2010), whenever possible the psychologist should avoid multiple relationships that might impair objectivity. Furthermore, as addressed earlier, the DoD has instructed BSCT members to separate such activities in all but the most emergent situations (e.g., active suicidality or psychotic behavior in the absence of alternative mental health care options), as articulated in *Medical Program Support for Detainee Operations* (DoD, 2006b) and MEDCOM *Behavioral Science Consultation Policy* (DA OTSG, 2010).

To defuse this potential conflict, psychologists who function as BSCT members are recommended to clarify their roles early on and to explain the need for separation of duties to their interrogation teams (Johnson, 1995; Staal & King, 2000). Moreover, they should ensure that there is a medical or mental health provider available to conduct such health-care-related evaluations as they arise. In such situations BSCT members would relay their concerns to a designated neutral party. This individual would then make the referral to medical support element personnel who would be able to directly address the psychological concerns of the detainee.

Scenario 2: Sharing Mental Health Information With Interrogation Teams

In the previous scenario, the BSCT psychologist was successful in deferring the mental status exam to a medical provider. After the interrogation support and health care roles had been adequately separated, the BSCT psychologist was asked to find out the results of the evaluation and pass them along to the interrogation team for further guidance. Although the BSCT psychologist initially indicated to the team leader that he needed to remain separated from any medical information (to include the mental status evaluation documented in the detainee's medical files), he was asked to reconsider because "you understand that psycho-babble stuff anyway, doc, and you can translate it into what the team needs to know." The BSCT psychologist remembered that detainee medical information would not routinely be provided to interrogators except for reasons of protecting health and welfare and that procedures existed regarding disclosure of that information. In this scenario, once the detainee medical team had evaluated the detainee and provided whatever treatment might have been indicated, the detainee was released for interrogation without limitations. The BSCT psychologist felt certain the detainee had been malingering and that this would become readily apparent to the interrogation team.

The BSCT psychologist wondered whether he should confirm the team's suspicions that the detainee was "faking it"? Did he need additional information from the medical team in order to confirm those suspicions? Moreover, would he be negligent not conveying information that a detainee was malingering, perhaps wasting time that could be used for gathering vital intelligence and only serving to aggravate the intelligence team the psychologist supports? Finally, was there any reason for the psychologist to remove himself from further contributions to this detainee's case?

Here the situation and clarification of rule are more complex. The BSCT psychologist first considers Standard 3.05, Multiple Relationships, of the Ethics Code (APA, 2010) and PENS Statement 6 (APA PENS, 2005; see Appendix) which states that "psychologists are sensitive to the problems inherent in mixing potentially inconsistent roles such as health care provider and consultant to an interrogation, and refrain from engaging in such multiple relationships." In this instance the BSCT psychologist would be functioning only as a consultant to the interrogation team and would not be evaluating the detainee's mental health status; hence he would not be entering a multiple relationship or mixing inconsistent roles.

The DoD and the DA (the branch of service that serves as the executive agent for interrogation and detention operations) agree that medical information cannot be used to the detriment of detainees (DA OTSG, 2010; DoD, 2006b). This is consistent with PENS Statement 3 (APA PENS, 2005). Further, DoD and DA, analogous to the civilian sector, outline procedures for disclosure of detainee medical information for purposes other than treatment. "Similar to legal standards applicable to U.S. citizens, permissible purposes include preventing harm to any person, maintaining public health and order in detention facilities, and any lawful law enforcement, intelligence, or national security-related activity" (DoD, 2006b, p. 3). On reflection, the BSCT psychologist decided he did not need any additional information from the medical team, having been informed that the detainee had been evaluated and cleared for interrogation. He decided to consider his suspicions as only one of several possible explanations for the detainee's behavior. The BSCT psychologist proceeded to consult with the interrogation team, knowing that the detainee would be treated humanely and that the team would follow applicable laws and conventions.

Scenario 3: Providing Mental Health Care to a Guard

In this scenario the BSCT psychologist has been working in a theater detention facility for several months and has established a strong rapport with the guards and interrogators. Moreover, he has been found to be reliable and trustworthy, a member of the team whom the intelligence commanders have relied on more and more. As a result, one of the guards has come to him for consultation on a personal problem. In the past, the psychologist has provided advice and education on various issues to staff members, but the guard's request is clearly personal in nature.

Knowing that he should attempt to avoid multiple relationships whenever possible (Ethical Standard 3.05, PENS Statement 6) and that he should not routinely provide behavioral health care to staff he supports (DA OTSG, 2010), the BSCT psychologist initially explains to the guard that it is best if he refers him to a mental health professional outside the facility. Unfortunately, given the austere location, the BSCT psychologist appears to be the only mental health provider in the immediate area. Moreover, the guard indicates that he will only trust the facility psychologist, stating, "I'll talk to you, doc, but not some shrink I don't know." The BSCT psychologist decides to consult with a peer who has worked in such operations in the past. In doing so, he is directed to recent published policies that indicate it is appropriate for BSCT psychologists, when other resources are unavailable or in emergent situations, to provide services to facility staff, although they do not routinely provide such care (DA OTSG, 2010; Johnson, 1995; Staal & King, 2000).

Scenario 4: Reporting Potential Abuse

A guard was overheard making a threat to a prisoner by a fellow guard who suggested that he consult the BSCT psychologist who works in the same detention facility. During the interview, the guard informs the psychologist that the detainee has been defecating and urinating on the floor of his cell rather than using the toilet. The guard states that the detainee has been doing this for several days and is tired of having to clean up after him. In a moment of anger the guard yelled at the detainee and threatened that if he did it one more time he was going to rub his face in the feces. The interview reveals that the guard had been working long hours and was experiencing some marital stress due to the year-long deployment. After making some additional inquiries, the BSCT psychologist determined that there were no cultural or other reasons for the detainee's behavior. Should the psychologist report this guard for punishment? How should the psychologist proceed?

As mentioned previously, the BSCT psychologist's central charter is to consult on the safe, legal, ethical, and effective implementation of the facilities interrogation and detention operations. In this case, at least three of the four elements of that charter may be in question. For example, threatening the detainee may place both the detainee and the guard in an unsafe situation, and as a violation of the facility's policies (and potentially other guidance such as the Geneva Conventions) it is behavior that may be deemed illegal. In addition, such threats may incense other detainees, causing disruption in the camp, which places both detainees and guards at risk, as well as increasing the detainees' resistance posture under interrogation, rendering the interrogations less effective. Not only do local procedures and DA policies require intervention to prevent possible harm, so too, do ethical principles require psychologists to "minimize harm where it is foreseeable" (i.e., Standard 3.04, Avoiding Harm; APA, 2010). Therefore, the BSCT psychologist is mandated to intervene, however, at what level may remain a judgment call. It is likely to be a multifaceted action.

At a minimum, the psychologist should encourage the guard to report what happened to his supervisors who can channel that information up the chain of command and document the incident accordingly. The psychologist may be mandated to report the information to the interrogation team so they can anticipate how the incident may impact their work with the detainee. In this case, the psychologist may decide to provide some additional training to the guard force on the principles of moral disengagement and behavioral drift. Such training is typical and often is illustrated using classic psychology research such as Milgram's (compliance with authority; Milgram, 1963) and Zimbardo's (Stanford prison; Zimbardo, 1971) studies. Examining the systemic causes behind the guard's behavior in this case may also prove valuable to the facility's leadership. This in turn may open the dialogue to shift schedules, morale, deployment rotations, and other personnel management issues that could have a positive impact on the overall stress levels of the detention facility staff. It is often in the area of education and training that BSCT members can help interrogation and detention operations personnel. For actual clinical support or stress management interventions, facility staff members would be referred to medical support personnel whenever possible.

Scenario 5: Limits of Competence

A clinical psychologist deployed to Iraq is assigned to the combat stress control detachment that provides behavioral health care to U.S. personnel working in that theater of operations. Predeployment training included the combat and operational stress control course. During the deployment the detachment was tasked with temporarily providing care at a detention facility during an underlap in medical personnel assignment to the facility. During the month that the psychologist has been providing care at the facility, he has only treated U.S. personnel and has not been called on to treat or evaluate detainees. The detention facility commander then asks the psychologist to provide consultation regarding the interrogation of a known terrorist who had just been taken into custody after he claimed responsibility for the kidnapping of three Red Cross workers and a U.S. journalist.

The psychologist here is not faced with issues of conflict of interest or dual relationships as were the BSCT personnel described in previous scenarios. He has treated neither the interrogator nor the detainee in question and does not have mental health information that might be revealed if he were to consult on the interrogation process. Neither is he concerned about potential abuse or mistreatment of the detainee. The psychologist is aware from his many conversations with guards, interrogators, and command staff that a strong program of risk management and oversight has been implemented to ensure that every detainee is treated in accordance with Geneva Conventions and is treated in a humane and respectful manner regardless of the reason for detention. He was provided a familiarization lecture on BSCT operations prior to deployment and believes that he understands the mission and objectives of personnel working in this capacity; however, he did not participate in the DA's official BSCT training course.

In this scenario the primary dilemma surrounds the issue of competence to perform the duties the psychologist has been asked to do. Adding to the complexity of the scenario is the issue of potential conflict between ethics and law, regulations, governing legal authority, and organizational demands. These issues are addressed in Ethical Standards 1.02, Conflicts Between Ethics and Law, Regulations, or Other Governing Legal Authority; 1.03, Conflicts Between Ethics and Organizational Demands; and 2.01, Boundaries of Competence (APA, 2010).

As detailed in chapter 1, at its February 2010 meeting, the APA Council of Representatives voted to amend Standards 1.02 and 1.03 in order to clearly communicate the Council's 2009 resolution that "Ethical Standards 1.02 and 1.03 can never be interpreted to justify or defend violating human rights." The amendments became effective June 1, 2010 (APA, 2010). They resolve any discrepancy with the statement in the Ethics Code's Introduction and Applicability section that "If psychologists' ethical responsibilities conflict with law, regulations, or other governing legal code, psychologists make known their commitment to the Ethics Code and take steps to resolve the conflict in a responsible manner in keeping with the basic principles of human rights."

As a military officer the psychologist is required to follow lawful orders of his superior officers, yet he is also expected to advise his commander of any potentially negative implications of following that order or any ethical or moral issues following that order would create for him. Ethical Standard 2.01, Boundaries of Competence, states that "psychologists provide services . . .

in areas only within the boundaries of their competence, based on their education, training, supervised experience, consultation, study, or professional experience" (APA, 2010). Furthermore, there are various DoD directives and instructions as well as the MEDCOM policy that delineate training requirements for personnel engaged in interrogation support. The psychologist in this scenario received familiarization training on this mission; he did not receive the requisite training for psychologists providing behavioral science consultation to interrogation operations.

Both the Ethics Code and the MEDCOM policy delineate the steps that the psychologist should take to resolve this dilemma; both require the psychologist to first talk with the commander issuing the instruction. Ethical Standard 1.03, Conflicts Between Ethics and Organizational Demands, advises the psychologist to clarify the nature of the conflict and attempt to resolve the conflict in a way that permits adherence to the Ethics Code. MEDCOM policy instructs the behavioral science consultants to "regularly monitor their behavior and remain within professional ethical boundaries as established by their professional associations, by their licensing State, and by the military" (DA OTSG, 2010, p. 6). The policy goes on to delineate the steps the psychologist in this scenario might take:

> Behavioral science personnel will not perform any duties they believe are illegal, immoral, or unethical. If behavioral science personnel feel they have been ordered to perform such duties, they should voice their concerns to and seek clarification from the chain of command. If the chain of command is unable to resolve the situation, BSCs [behavioral science consultants] should seek alternate means of resolution by contacting their Specialty Consultant and/or the OTSG BSC SME [subject matter expert]. As always, other mechanisms, such as the Inspector General, criminal investigation organizations, or Judge Advocates, also may be used. (DA OTSG, 2010, pp. 10–11)

Thus, the psychologist in this scenario who is unprepared to fulfill the role of behavioral science consultant, by virtue of training and experience, has several courses of action and recourse, as delineated in both the Ethics Code and military policy, to resolve the conflict.

SUMMARY AND CONCLUSIONS

Psychologists are increasingly being called on to engage in activities that directly support national security. Although this is not a new practice, it has expanded significantly following the events of September 11, 2001. This increasing inclusion of psychologists into intelligence communities and military operational activities has brought with it a variety of concerns and controversies. We have attempted in this chapter to illuminate the relevant law, published policies and military doctrine, and the associated ethical standards that provide guidance to psychologists engaged in such activities, specifically in support of the interrogation and detention of enemy combatants. In doing so, we have also highlighted a number of areas that will benefit from further discussion and debate.

For example, how can individual psychologists and the professional association best support application of sound scientific principles as a foundation for national security activities (Fein et al., 2006; see also Borum, Fein, Vossekuil, Gelles, & Shumate, 2004)? What is the appropriate level of training needed for psychologists who wish to engage in such operational support roles? What constitutes competence in these areas? Should this area of practice be acknowledged or certified by outside organizations such as the American Board of Professional Psychology or the APA's Commission for Recognition of Specialties and Proficiencies in Professional Psychology as its own specialty (Gelles, 2007; Stephenson & Staal, 2007b)? What role do psychologists have in fostering an environment of scientific inquiry into training requirements, effectiveness, and best practices for interrogators and those professionals who provide behavioral science consultation to interrogations and other national security operations? How can the larger community of psychologists and other professionals best support their colleagues practicing behavioral science consultation to intelligence collection and detention operations and other areas of operational psychology (Baughman & Dorsey, 2009)?

The United States and the APA have made it clear that psychologists will not support activities that involve torture or result in inhuman and/or degrading treatment. As discussed in previous sections of this chapter, federal law and military doctrine are consistent with Geneva Conventions and the APA policy in their insistence on humane treatment of detained persons and their prohibitions against torture and other cruel, inhuman, and degrading punishment. It may be expected that many questions and issues remain unresolved; it may also be expected that psychologists will continue to support national security activities (see Lowman, 2009, for a fuller discussion of these activities).

Although some will weigh the issues and choose not to practice in areas of national security, others will recognize the unique contribution they may make in these roles and accept the responsibility to apply their expertise and moral compass in this challenging area of practice (APA PENS, 2005; Civiello, 2009; Greene & Banks, 2009; James, 2008). In so doing, one may expect that psychologists engaged in these activities will continue to struggle with decisions about their professional behavior, weighing competing positive values, and that they will continue to bring these questions to the APA as they have in the past.

Although

in the abstract the APA code of ethics places no heavier value on our obligations to individuals than our obligations to society in general, . . . [it] provides ample room for disagreement among reasonable professionals regarding the weight to be placed on an individual's rights and society's interests in regulating our own conduct. (Grisso, 2001, pp. 459–460)

We believe that open dialogue with psychologists engaged in national security activities about the dilemmas they face, coordination with supporting organizations and governing bodies, guideline development, and informing this process with knowledge and expertise of those doing the actual work will ensure that the delivery of psychological services in this emerging area of practice continues to meet the highest ethical and professional standards.

REFERENCES

American Academy of Psychiatry and the Law. (2005). *Ethics guidelines for the practice of forensic psychiatry*. Retrieved December 8, 2009, from http://www.aapl.org/pdf/ethicsgdlns.pdf

American Medical Association Council on Ethical and Judicial Affairs. (2006). *Physician participation in interrogation*. Retrieved June 6, 2008, from http://www.ama-assn.org/ama1/pub/upload/mm/38/a-06ceja.pdf

American Psychiatric Association. (2006). *Psychiatric participation in interrogation of detainees: Position statement*. Retrieved December 8, 2009, from http://archive.psych.org/edu/other_res/lib_archives/archives/200601.pdf

American Psychological Association. (2009). *Psychologists and unlawful detention settings with a focus on national security*. Retrieved January 15, 2010, from http://www.apa.org/about/governance/council/09feb-crminutes.aspx

American Psychological Association. (2010). *Ethical principles of psychologists and code of conduct (2002, Amended June 1, 2010)*. Retrieved from http://www.apa.org/ethics/code/index.aspx

American Psychological Association, Presidential Task Force on Ethics and National Security. (2005). *Report of the American Psychological Association Presidential Task Force on Psychological Ethics and National Security*. Retrieved December 8, 2009, from http://www.apa.org/releases/PENSTaskForceReportFinal.pdf

Bandura, A. (1986). *Social foundations of thought and action: A social cognitive theory*. Englewood Cliffs, NJ: Prentice Hall.

Bandura, A., Barbaranelli, C., Caprara, G. V., & Pastorelli, C. (1996). Mechanisms of moral disengagement in the exercise of moral agency. *Journal of Personality and Social Psychology, 71*, 364–374.

Baughman, W. A., & Dorsey, D. W. (2009). Consulting psychology and the intelligence community: Toward a new support paradigm. *Consulting Psychology Journal: Practice and Research, 61*, 56–67.

Behnke, S. (2006, July–August). Ethics and interrogations: Comparing and contrasting the American Psychological, American Medical and American Psychiatric Association positions. *Monitor on Psychology, 37*, 66–7.

Borum, R., Fein, R., Vossekuil, B., Gelles, M., & Shumate, S. (2004). The role of operational research in counterterrorism. *International Journal of Intelligence 17*, 420–434. (Also available from http://works.bepress.com/randy_borum/8)

Borum, R., Gelles, M., & Kleinman, S. (2009). Interview and interrogation: A perspective and update from the USA (draft version). In R. Milne, S. Savage, & T. Williamson (Eds.), *International developments in investigative interviewing*. Cullomtpon, Devon, England: Willan Publishing. Retrieved December 11, 2009, from http://works.bepress.com/cgi/viewcontent.cgi?article=1043&context=randy_borum

Britt, S. H., & Morgan, J. D. (1946). Military psychologists in World War II. *American Psychologist, 1*, 423–437.

Civiello, C. L. (2009). Introduction to the special issue on organizational consulting in national security contexts. *Consulting Psychology Journal: Practice and Research, 61*, 1–4.

Detainee Treatment Act of 2005, Pub. L. No. 109-248, Title X (2006).

Detert, J. R., Trevino, L. K., & Sweitzer, V. L. (2008). Moral disengagement in ethical decision making: A study of antecedents and outcomes. *Journal of Applied Psychology, 93*, 374–391.

Fein, R. A., Lehner, P., & Vossekuil, B. (2006). *Educing information—Interrogation: Science and art, foundations for the future*. Retrieved December 8, 2009, from http://www.dtic.mil/cgi-bin/GetTRDoc?AD=ADA476636&Location=U2&doc=GetTRDoc.pdf

Gelles, M. (2007). *Board certification in clinical psychology for national security operational psychologists (ABPP): Core operational knowledge*. Unpublished manuscript.

Greene, C. H., & Banks, L. M. (2009). Ethical guideline evolution in psychological support to interrogation operations. *Consulting Psychology Journal: Practice and Research, 61*, 25–32.

Grisso, T. (2001). Reply to Schafer: Doing harm ethically. *Journal of the American Academy of Psychiatry and the Law, 29*, 457–460.

Haney, C., Banks, C., & Zimbardo, P. (1973) A study of prisoners and guards in a simulated prison. *Naval Research Review, 30*, 4–17

Hannah, G., Clutterbuck, L., & Rubin, J. (2008). *Radicalization or rehabilitation: Understanding the challenge of extremist and radicalized prisoners*. Retrieved December 27, 2009, from http://www.rand.org/pubs/technical_reports/TR571/

James, L. C. (2008). *Fixing hell: An Army psychologist confronts Abu Ghraib*. New York: Grand Central.

Johnson. W. B. (1995). Perennial ethical quandaries in military psychology: Toward American Psychological Association–Department of Defense collaboration. *Professional Psychology: Research and Practice, 26*, 281–287.

Johnson, W. B. (2008). Top ethical challenges for military clinical psychologists. *Military Psychology, 20*, 49–62.

Layman, J. W. (1943). Utilization of clinical psychologists in the general hospitals of the Army. *Psychological Bulletin, 40*, 212–216.

Lowman, R. L. (Ed.). (2009). Organizational consulting in national security contexts [Special issue]. *Consulting Psychology Journal: Practice and Research, 61*(1).

McAlister, A. L., Bandura, A., & Owen, S. V. (2006). Mechanisms of moral disengagement in support of military force: The impact of Sept. 11. *Journal of Social and Clinical Psychology, 25*, 141–165.

McGuire, F. L. (1990). *Psychology aweigh: A history of clinical psychology in the United States Navy, 1900–1988.* Washington, DC: American Psychological Association.

Melton, A. W. (1957). Military psychology in the United States of America. *American Psychologist, 12*, 740–746.

Milgram, S. (1963). Behavioral study of obedience. *Journal of Abnormal and Social Psychology, 67*, 371–378.

Monahan, J. (1980). *Who is the client? The ethics of psychological intervention in the criminal justice system.* Washington, DC: American Psychological Association.

Picano, J. J., Roland, R. R., Rollins, K. D., & Williams, T. J. (2002). Personality correlates of staff and peer ratings in operational assessment. *Proceedings of the annual conference of the International Military Testing Association, Australia*, pp. 191–195. Retrieved May 25, 2009, from http://www.internationalmta.org/Documents/2001/Proceedings2001.pdf

Rahe, R. H., & Genender, E. (1983). Adaptation to and recovery from captivity stress. *Military Medicine, 148*, 577–585.

Shumate, S., & Borum, R. (2006). Psychological support to defense counterintelligence operations. *Military Psychology, 18*, 283–296. (Also available from http://works.bepress.com/cgi/viewcontent.cgi?article=1008&context=randy_borum)

Shumate, S., Borum, R., Turner, J., & Fogarty, J. L. (2006). Middle Eastern mindset: Operational analysis and implications. *American Intelligence Journal, 24*, 45–55. (Also available from http://works.bepress.com/randy_borum/37)

Staal, M. A., & King, R. E. (2000). Managing a multiple relationship environment: The ethics of military psychology. *Professional Psychology: Research and Practice, 31*, 698–705.

Staal, M. A., & Stephenson, J. A. (2006). Operational psychology: An emerging subdiscipline in psychology. *Military Psychology, 18*, 269–282.

Stephenson, J. A., & Staal, M. A. (2007a). An ethical decision-making model for operational psychology. *Ethics & Behavior, 17*, 61–82.

Stephenson, J. A., & Staal, M. A. (2007b). Operational psychology: What constitutes expertise? *The Specialist, 26*, 30–31.

United Nations Office of the High Commissioner for Human Rights. (1949). *Geneva convention relative to the protection of civilian persons in time of war: Part 1, Article 3.* Retrieved July 31, 2007, from http://www.unhchr.ch/html/menu3/b/92.htm

U.S. Department of the Army. (1956). *The law of land warfare* (FM-27-10). Retrieved June 5, 2008, from http://www.globalsecurity.org/military/library/policy/army/fm/27-10/

U.S. Department of the Army Headquarters. (2006). *Human intelligence collector operations* FM 2-22.3 (previously FM 34-52). Retrieved June 5, 2008, from http://www.army.mil/institution/armypublicaffairs/pdf/fm2-22-3.pdf

U.S. Department of the Army Office of the Surgeon General. (2006). *Behavioral Science consultation policy* (OTSG/MEDCOM Policy Memo 06-029). Washington, DC: Author.

U. S. Department of the Army Office of the Surgeon General. (2010). *Behavioral science consultation policy* (OTSG/MEDCOM Policy Memo 09-053). Washington, DC: Author.

U.S. Department of Defense. (2005). *DoD intelligence interrogations, detainee debriefings, and tactical questioning* (DoD Directive No. 3115.09). Retrieved June 7, 2008, from http://www.dtic.mil/whs/directives/corres/pdf/311509p.pdf

U.S. Department of Defense. (2006a). *The Department of Defense detainee program* (DoD Directive No. 2310.01E). Retrieved June 7, 2008, from http://www.defense link.mil/pubs/pdfs/Detainee_Prgm_Dir_2310_9-5-06.pdf

U.S. Department of Defense. (2006b). *Medical program support for detainee operations* (DoD Instruction No. 2310.08E). Retrieved June 7, 2008, from http://www.dtic.mil/whs/directives/corres/pdf/231008p.pdf

U.S. Department of Defense Health Affairs. (2005) *Medical program principles and procedures for the protection and treatment of detainees in the custody of the armed forces of the United States* (HA Policy: 05-006). Retrieved June 7, 2008, from http://www1.umn.edu/humanrts/OathBetrayed/Winkenwerder%206-3-2005.pdf

U.S. Department of Justice Office of Legal Counsel. (2002). *Standards of conduct for interrogation under 18 U.S.C. §§ 2340-2340A.* Retrieved June 6, 2008, from http://www.washingtonpost.com/wp-srv/nation/documents/dojinterrogationmemo20020801.pdf

U.S. Department of Justice Office of Legal Counsel. (2004). *Legal standards applicable under 18 U.S.C. §§ 2340-2340A.* Retrieved June 6, 2008, from http://www.usdoj.gov/olc/18usc23402340a2.htm

Williams, T. J., Picano, J. J., Roland, R. R., & Banks, L. M. (2006). Introduction to operational psychology. In C. H. Kennedy & E. A. Zillmer (Eds.), *Military psychology: Clinical and operational applications* (pp. 193–214). New York: Guilford Press.

Zimbardo, P. G. (1971). The power and pathology of imprisonment. *Congressional Record.* (Serial No. 15, October 25, 1971). Hearings before Subcommittee No. 3 of the Committee on the Judiciary, House of Representatives, 92d Cong,, *First Session on Corrections, Part II, Prisons, Prison Reform and Prisoner's Rights: California.* Washington, DC: U.S. Government Printing Office.

6

ETHICS IN CRISIS NEGOTIATION: A LAW ENFORCEMENT AND PUBLIC SAFETY PERSPECTIVE

MICHAEL G. GELLES AND RUSSELL PALAREA

Historically, hostage taking is a phenomenon that has been around for centuries. In many cases, formal negotiation models did not evolve until the early 1970s. The origins of hostage negotiation and the role of psychological consultation can be linked to the tragic incident at the 1972 Olympic Games when 11 Israeli athletes were taken hostage and subsequently murdered (Schreiber, 1973). Following that incident, in 1973, the New York City Police Department and the Federal Bureau of Investigation (FBI) instituted a hostage negotiations training program to train police officers around the world. The first involvement of a psychologist in hostage negotiations can be traced to the 1970s when Harvey Schlossberg, a detective with a doctorate in psychology, and Frank Boltz, a police lieutenant, began developing a model for negotiations that was built around psychological principles and was sensitive to understanding personality, behavior, emotions, and motivation (McMains & Mullins, 1996). As a result of Schlossberg's pioneering work, the role of the psychologist in supporting hostage negotiations has continued to evolve. The key to the success of the

The views expressed in this article are those of the authors and do not reflect the official policy or position of the U.S. Department of the Navy, U.S. Department of Defense, or the U.S. Government.

107

psychologist's role has been in providing insight into the motivations and mental health issues of the hostage taker by serving as consultant to hostage negotiation teams in the field (Rowe, Gelles, & Palarea, 2006).

Although the roles, responsibilities, and functions of psychologists consulting on crisis negotiations are well documented (see Rowe et al., 2006), ethical guidelines for consulting on this mission have yet to be established. Consulting on crisis negotiations brings about a variety of ethical challenges, and the need for ethical guidelines is clear. By the nature of the task, the psychologist is placed into a conflict between the needs of the law enforcement agency (the psychologist's client) to provide public safety, the needs of any persons taken hostage, and the needs of the individual in crisis (in this instance, the hostage taker). Addressing these often competing responsibilities can be challenging, but the importance of effectively operating in this environment using clear ethical guidelines is paramount.

PSYCHOLOGY AND CRISIS NEGOTIATIONS: A NATURAL PARTNERSHIP

The model developed by Schlossberg and Boltz demonstrates the partnership between psychologists and crisis negotiation teams. Their techniques emphasize containment and negotiation with the hostage taker, understanding the hostage taker's motivation and personality, and slowing down the incident so time can benefit the negotiator (Schlossberg, 1979). These incidents are viewed as crises for the individual initiating the incident and treated accordingly whenever possible, and Schlossberg's work demonstrated the utility of on-scene psychological consultation. The hostage takers involved in these situations often experience psychotic, mood, substance abuse or dependence, or personality disorder symptoms or heightened emotional states. Psychologists assist the police with understanding the subject's mind-set and the role of any mental illnesses, interpreting the subject's behavior, and developing communication strategies. More recently, psychologists have applied operational risk assessment models (e.g., behavioral-based threat assessment; Borum, Fein, Vossekuil, & Berglund, 1999; Fein & Vossekuil, 1998) to assist the police in determining the subject's risk for violence.

Within this realm, psychologists serve as consultants to the negotiation team. Although some psychologists have been asked to move from a consultation role into a negotiation role, this blending of roles is strongly discouraged. By serving as the negotiator, the psychologist may become preoccupied with fulfilling the negotiator's duties and lose the consultant's objectivity, thus diminishing the value of his or her psychological expertise to the negotiation team. The psychologist also enters into an inappropriate dual relationship with the individual in crisis and in the midst of a potential tactical intervention creates a variety of unnecessary ethical problems.

PSYCHOLOGISTS' DUTIES IN CRISIS NEGOTIATIONS

Before we enter into a discussion of the ethics of psychological consultation to crisis negotiations, we first review the duties that psychologists fulfill in this mission. The knowledge, skills, and training possessed by clinical psychologists provide the foundation for operational application to crisis negotiations. Clinical psychologists are well suited to consult on issues involving subjects' mental state, patterns of behavior, and risk for violence. In addition to these on-scene consultation issues, there are a number of other duties that psychologists can provide to crisis negotiations. Rowe et al. (2006) identified these duties in terms of preincident, intraincident, and postincident phases (see Exhibit 6.1).

EXHIBIT 6.1
Psychologists' Duties During the Three Phases of Crisis Negotiations

Preincident duties

    Provide psychological screening and selection of negotiators.

    Provide training on psychological topics (e.g., active listening skills, persuasion techniques, crisis intervention, assessment of personality types, threat and violence risk assessment).

    Participate in training exercises (see Fuselier, 1981).

Intraincident duties

    Monitor the negotiations; translate the communications and behavior of the subject.

    Manage the stress level of the negotiator.

    Liaise with collateral sources and other professionals to support the ongoing assessment of the subject.

    Assist negotiators in the management of the subject's behaviors that are presented during the negotiation (e.g., psychiatric disorders, triggers to agitation).

    Assess the interface between the mental state of the subject and the unfolding situation.

    Assess the original motivation for the barricade situation and the evolving motivations underlying each communication.

    Analyze intelligence gathered through interviews with family members and other data sources regarding the subject's patterns of behaviors and violence risk.

    Apply the behavioral-based threat assessment model (Borum, Fein, Vossekuil, & Berglund, 1999; Fein & Vossekuil, 1998) to determine if the subject is *making* and/or *posing* a threat and moving toward violence.

Postincident duties

    Provide stress management education.

    Provide team debriefings and counseling to crisis team members; however, clinical duties such as debriefing and counseling should be conducted by a second psychologist who is not a member of the crisis negotiation team to avoid a dual relationship ethical conflict.

It is important to understand that there are two intraincident phases to a crisis situation: the *negotiation* phase and the *tactical* phase. The psychologist only participates in the negotiation phase. The goal of the negotiation phase is to achieve a peaceful resolution to the situation with no loss of life to the hostages, the perpetrator, or the police. The psychologist consults to the police during the negotiation phase, but the intraincident psychological consultation ends when the commanding police officer decides to move from negotiation to tactical resolution.

Furthermore, it is critical to understand the limitations of the psychologist's role in operational consultations such as crisis negotiations. As a consultant, the psychologist assesses and interprets information for operational use by the law enforcement professional (in this case, the crisis negotiation team) with the goal of bringing about a peaceful end to the crisis (e.g., an individual threatening suicide) or the hostage situation. The psychologist does not serve as a treating clinician for the hostage taker and has no direct contact with that individual. The psychologist also has no function in the determination of ending the negotiation phase and shifting to a tactical intervention.

Finally, regarding postincident duties, it is recommended that clinical and operational psychology roles be kept separate from each other. The psychologist who provides operational consultation services to negotiators functions as a member of the negotiation team; therefore, the operational psychologist does not maintain the objectivity to then serve in a clinical debrief or counseling role for that same team. Doing so may not only constitute a violation of the American Psychological Association's (APA's) "Ethical Principles of Psychologists and Code of Conduct" (Ethics Code) on multiple relationships (Ethical Standard 3.05; APA, 2010) but also has the potential to prevent the psychologist from engaging in appropriate self-care or help seeking when necessary. Thus, we recommend that a separate psychologist be brought in to conduct postincident clinical debriefs, including debriefing the operational psychologist, and provide any necessary clinical services to the negotiation team members.

APPLYING THE APA ETHICS CODE

Although the Ethics Code (APA, 2010) was not written specifically with crisis negotiation in mind, several sections are relevant to crisis negotiations. Before we enter into a discussion of the applications of the Ethics Code to crisis negotiations, we note the importance of the interplay and subsequent conflicts that arise among the Ethics Code (APA, 2010), individual state laws, and the operational demands faced by psychologists consulting in crisis negotiations. Standard 1.02 of the APA Ethics Code states, "If psychologists' ethical responsibilities conflict with law, regulations, or other governing legal authority, psychologists clarify the nature of the conflict, make known their commitment to the Ethics Code and take reasonable steps to resolve the conflict consistent with the General Principles and Ethical Standards of the Ethics Code. Under no circumstances may this standard be used to justify or defend violating human rights." (APA, 2010). This wording reflects the most recent amendment to the Standard, approved by the APA Council of Representatives in February 2010 as detailed in chapter 1, and effective June 1, 2010 (APA, 2010).

Standard 1.03, which was similarly amended, notes,

> If the demands of an organization with which psychologists are affiliated or for whom they are working are in conflict with this Ethics Code, psychologists clarify the nature of the conflict, make known their commitment to the Ethics Code, and take reasonable steps to resolve the conflict consistent with the General Principles and Ethical Standards of the Ethics Code. Under no circumstances may this standard be used to justify or defend violating human rights. (APA, 2010)

Psychologists who provide operational consultation on crisis negotiations must be intimately familiar with the Ethics Code and the laws that govern their practice before entering into a crisis negotiation consultation. Given the high stress and high demand environment of the negotiation scene, it is probable that the operational psychologist will be placed into an ethical conflict by a request made by the negotiation team, the law enforcement agency's senior leadership, or the negotiation situation itself. Thus, it is imperative that the operational psychologist anticipate, identify, and resolve potential ethical conflicts and educate the negotiation team and senior leadership on the appropriate use and limitations of the psychological consultation.

In applying the Ethics Code (APA, 2010) to crisis negotiations, the ethical considerations fall into five general categories: (a) specific applications to crisis negotiations, (b) indirect assessment issues, (c) training and competency issues, (d) considerations in consulting with law enforcement, and (e) additional considerations.

Specific Applications to Crisis Negotiation

Psychologists who engage in this practice must be aware of the ethical codes that are relevant to crisis negotiations.

Ethical Standard 3.11, Psychological Services Delivered to or Through Organizations

The foremost issue in crisis negotiation consultation lies in establishing the identification of the client, the psychologist's role and services provided, and the roles of other individuals at the crisis scene. This question has been a core ethical issue since psychologists began developing consultation roles within the criminal justice system (see Monahan, 1980 for an in-depth discussion on this issue). In this situation, the client is the law enforcement agency to whom the psychologist provides consultation. The client is not the hostage taker or the hostages, though the psychologist's purpose is to assist in the facilitation of a resolution that preserves the life of each individual involved in the situation (see the section that follows on Ethics Code Standard 3.04, Avoiding Harm).

The role of the psychologist on the crisis negotiation team has evolved and become more defined over time (McMains & Mullins, 1996). Because Schlossberg (1979) was a psychologist and a police detective, his model was developed from the operational perspective of applying psychological principles to crisis negotiation situations. This thrust differs from the traditional role of police psychologists, who provide clinical services to officers.

For a psychologist serving on a negotiation team, differentiating between the clinical and operational roles is critical. The two roles must be kept separate; they have very different functions with different ethical challenges. This separation of roles establishes expectations and manages ambiguity of roles during the negotiation process. It also provides the psychologist a guideline for what his or her role does and does not involve during the negotiation, thus ensuring the psychologist engages in roles that represent consulting psychologists' competencies as well as the profession's ethical values (Handelsman, Knapp, & Gottlieb, 2002).

The potential for blurring the line of separation between clinical and operational duties may come from the operational psychologist or the police officers on the negotiation team. The operational psychologist may slide into a clinical role out of desire or habit. Alternatively, the officers may turn to the operational psychologist for clinical support because they know he or she is also a clinical psychologist, and an established trusting relationship already exists. To avoid such situations, it is important that the operational psychologist clearly define his or her role with the negotiation team before a crisis situation arises especially because clinical and operational roles may be blurred as a result of the high stress and operational tempo at the crisis negotiation scene.

Consider the following example. A hostage taker was holding hostage three adults whom he had threatened to kill. The crisis negotiation team was deployed to the scene and included an operational psychologist. The operational psychologist's duties involved assessing the hostage taker's potential for violence and monitoring the effectiveness of the negotiators' communications. The psychologist noticed that over the course of the negotiation, the level of stress demonstrated by the negotiators was escalating rapidly. In response, the psychologist suggested that multiple negotiators take turns conducting the negotiation to obtain a "psychological breather." As the scenario unfolded, the hostage taker escalated the potential for violence through threats, and a hostage was executed. In an attempt to save additional lives, the commanding officer ordered a tactical response, and the hostage taker was killed. Following the incident, the negotiators wanted to debrief with the operational psychologist. Because the operational psychologist had not clearly defined his role with the team prior to the incident, he had to defer quickly and obtain support from a clinician who was not involved in the negotiation to conduct the debrief.

Ethical Standard 3.04, Avoiding Harm, and PENS Task Force Statement 11, Identifying the Client

Ethical Standard 3.04 (APA, 2010) makes it clear that although the law enforcement or government agency is the primary client, the psychologist has an obligation to other involved individuals. In the case of crisis negotiations, this means that in addition to the safety of law enforcement personnel, the psychologist has an obligation to the individual who has initiated the need for the crisis negotiation as well as any hostages or innocent bystanders.

For example, an attempted robbery is interrupted by a police officer who pulls into a gas station. The perpetrator panics, takes two individuals hostage, and threatens to kill them if the police officer does not back away from the gas station. A crisis negotiation team is sent to the scene. At the moment of his first interaction with team, the hostage taker demands that the police shoot him through the window in what is an apparent "suicide by cop" scenario (Mohandie & Meloy, 2000). The hostage taker is at the same time holding a hostage at gunpoint at the window. The negotiation team learns, through several brief interactions, that the hostage taker believes that he is the second disciple of Jesus Christ and must be assisted in his return to heaven. The team's operational psychologist assesses the degree of delusional thinking and suicidality to make an assessment of violence risk. As a result, the operational psychologist is able to provide direct consultation to the negotiators to assist in releasing the hostages. He encourages the hostage negotiators not to argue with the reality of the delusion and to appeal to the hostage taker's godly functions around not killing innocent people. The operational psychologist encourages the negotiators to be attentive to the subject's compromised mental state and to convince him that his actions are contrary to God's wishes and that his release of the hostages will enable the police to meet his wishes and assist his ascent to heaven. Eventually, the hostages are released. The commanding officer then decides to gain entry into the house with tear gas. The hostage taker is contained and transported to the hospital where he is committed for a psychiatric evaluation. Without the operational psychologist's input, the police might have interpreted the subject's actions only as threatening, which could have resulted in using a tactical response prematurely, and not only the hostage taker but also the hostages and possibly several police officers could have been killed.

Some may argue that having a psychologist actively consulting in a crisis negotiation is contrary to the psychology profession, particularly in a situation in which the police may injure or kill a hostage taker. However, the purpose of the operational psychologist is to assist the negotiation team in gaining insight into the perpetrator's mental health, motivations, and risk for violence in order to bring a peaceful resolution. The operational psychologist's consultation is provided to prevent the need for a tactical resolution, which may result in loss of life to the hostage taker, hostages, or police. The primary purpose of the psychologist consulting to crisis negotiations is to avoid harm and, subsequently, to preserve life.

Ethical Standard 2.06, Personal Problems and Conflicts

Crisis negotiation situations involve matters of life and death. To consult on these situations, the operational psychologist must be free of personal problems or conflicts that substantially impair his or her ability to consult in high-stress situations. If the operational psychologist is preoccupied or distracted or suffered a previous trauma and is unable to objectively monitor and provide feedback on the negotiation, the effects may be detrimental. It is also important for the operational psychologist to sort out his or her own moral perceptions (e.g., Fowers, 2005) to ensure he or she maintains awareness of the circumstances that may bring personal values into conflict with the ethical responsibilities demanded by the situation (Knapp, Gottlieb, Berman, & Handelsman, 2007).

Ethical Issues Involved With Indirect Assessments

Providing an assessment using only collateral and second hand data, and not having direct contact with the subject can be challenging and require some guidance and methodology to execute in the most reliable manner.

Ethical Standard 9.01, Bases for Assessments

Indirect assessment techniques have been demonstrated to be quite useful for psychologists who do not have direct access to the individual being assessed. The use of indirect assessment techniques in operational psychology dates back to World War II with the Office of Strategic Services' (predecessor to the CIA) assessment of Adolf Hitler (Williams, Picano, Roland, & Banks, 2006). Since then, indirect assessment techniques have been demonstrated to be useful in consulting with government agencies across a multitude of missions (Morgan et al., 2006). For example, indirect assessment techniques were subsequently used to develop psychological assessments of other political leaders, such as assessments of Anwar al-Sadat and Menachem Begin for President Carter's use in the Camp David Peace Accord negotiations (Post, 2004). Indirect assessment techniques have also been used in law enforcement contexts, such as in conducting psychological autopsies (Gelles, 1995) and threat assessments (Borum et al., 1999; Fein & Vossekuil, 1998).

What is most relevant to operational psychologists consulting to crisis negotiators is that they must formulate some opinion regarding a hostage taker and are required to use sources of data that do not come from a direct assessment. They must rely on what others say about the hostage taker and what can be derived from the communications between the hostage taker and negotiators. Additionally, there may be other sources of information, such as criminal records or family members who can provide additional insight into the hostage taker's level of functioning, emotional and physical state, motivation, cognitive style, and personality. Such information can be collected and analyzed by the operational psychologist to best develop an assessment of the hostage taker so that the team can interpret his or her communications and behaviors in the most reliable manner. The team can then use this psychological insight to make operational decisions in the course of the negotiations.

Within the crisis negotiation mission, the operational psychologist does not need direct interaction, either in person or on the phone, to conduct the psychological assessment. All of the information needed to conduct the assessment can be gathered through indirect means. Sources of information include public records, medical records, database checks, and interviews of family members, friends, coworkers, and neighbors. Additional information can be gathered through on-scene observations, such as assessing the subject's environment (i.e., the location of the standoff) and monitoring the communications between the subject and the negotiator (Rowe et al., 2006).

The use of indirect assessment methods requires special consideration. Psychologists who perform indirect assessments maintain an ethical responsibility to discuss their use and limitations with law enforcement officials. This is similar to what neuropsychologists encounter when explaining the reasoning and basis for the appropriateness of their use of a given assessment tool within the evaluation's context (cf., Bush & National Academy of Neuropsychology Policy and Planning Committee, 2005).

Ethical Standards 9.03, Informed Consent in Assessments, and 3.10, Informed Consent

Within a crisis negotiation, there is obviously no opportunity to gain the informed consent of the individual being assessed (i.e., the hostage taker). However, this should not preclude the psychologist from providing his or her expertise to this situation. Psychologists are able to render their expert opinion exclusively through indirect assessment means (Morgan et al., 2006).

Ethical Issues of Training and Competency

With the advent of operational psychology developing core competencies are critical and become a central ethical challenge. The psychologist must recognize that gaps exist in their core competencies in the area of consulting to negotiations.

Ethical Standards 2.01, Boundaries of Competence; 2.03, Maintaining Competence; and 2.02, Providing Services in Emergencies

The establishment of competence in psychological consultation to crisis negotiations is paramount. Before a psychologist serves as a member of the crisis team, he or she must receive general training in crisis negotiations, specific training in psychological consultation to crisis negotiators, and appropriate supervision. Although one could argue that Ethical Standard 2.02, Providing Services in Emergencies, allows psychologists to provide their services in emergency situations despite not having the proper training, we caution against applying this element of the code to crisis negotiations. Psychologists who do not have experience with operational consultation to law enforcement and who do not have specialized training in on-scene crisis negotiation consultation will be at risk of violating Ethical Standard 3.04, Avoiding Harm. Furthermore, practicing beyond the bounds of competence may constitute a violation of state law that could result in the removal of one's psychology license or other legal action.

The importance of receiving specialized training in psychological consultation to crisis negotiations cannot be overemphasized. Crisis negotiations involve matters of life and death; psychologists consulting to crisis negotiations must be knowledgeable about the dynamics, motivations, and nuances of the perpetrator's mind-set and the negotiation process. For example, a psychologist who lacks appropriate training in crisis negotiation may not correctly assess a subject's motivation for taking his children hostage. When the subject asks the negotiator to put his ex-wife on the phone, the untrained psychologist may not consider that this request presents an increased risk of violence because it may be the subject's intention to kill his children while his ex-wife listens to the shooting over the phone.

It is critical that psychologists consulting to crisis negotiators receive and maintain proper training in this field. Psychologists who will be consulting on a crisis negotiation mission should first take a negotiator's training class to understand the role and function of the negotiator. Additionally, they should undergo supervised training with an operational psychologist who is skilled in crisis negotiations. They should also receive training and mentoring in conducting indirect assessments and behaviorally based threat assessments and seek any other opportunities for field exposure to law enforcement investigations and operations. There are a variety of resources for crisis negotiation training, such as courses through police academies; the FBI; local, regional, and state police crisis negotiation associations; the IACP; and the Society of Police and Criminal Psychology. Information on training and links to local hostage negotiation association Web sites can be obtained through the International Association of Hostage Negotiators' Web site (http://www.hostagenegotiation.com). There is currently no formal certification for psychological consultation to crisis negotiations. Until such a certification process is established, the psychologist in training should seek approval from a supervising crisis negotiation psychologist to determine that he or she has the necessary competencies and supervised experience to consult independently.

Furthermore, psychologists should remain mindful of how individuals within various cultures and ethnicities may differ (cf., Manly & Jacobs, 2002) and should receive specialized training in cultural differences. As a result of the unique differences between cultures, there exists the potential for significant misinterpretation during the negotiation process. For example, individuals from different cultures process information differently. Consider the case of a hostage taker of Middle Eastern descent. One cultural element common to this geographic region is an associative, nonlinear cognitive style (Patai, 2007). The operational psychologist helped the negotiation team understand that the hostage taker's jumping from topic to topic was reflective of an associative thinking style as opposed to a decline in psychological and/or cognitive functioning. Additionally, the psychologist helped the negotiator formulate communications that would have the greatest ease of being understood by the subject, and in turn, worked with the negotiator on eliciting information that was accurate and reliable. If the operational psychologist had not been familiar with this cognitive style, he or she might have interpreted the subject's communication as a sign of a decompensating mental state. In turn, the commanding officer might have made the decision to shift to a tactical intervention when, in fact, the use of negotiation was still a viable option.

Considerations in Law Enforcement Consultation

Psychologists who consult to law enforcement agencies must be very sensitive to their role and function. They must be aware of the different relationships that exist within the organizations they serve and mindful of blurred roles and boundaries when consulting.

Ethical Standard 3.05, Multiple Relationships

As previously described, there are opportunities for operational and clinical psychology consultation in the crisis negotiation mission, although these roles must be clearly defined and remain independent of each other. As a member of the crisis negotiation team, the operational psychologist is embedded with team personnel and thus builds relationships with the other team members. The operational psychologist provides preincident training to the team members and provides the psychological consultation during the negotiation. Although this consultation activity fulfills an operational need, it precludes the psychologist from serving in a clinical role with the team members because doing so would constitute a violation of Ethical Standard 3.05a, Multiple Relationships. Operational psychologists who serve as members of a negotiation team must remain vigilant for such potential boundary violations. The operational psychologist who is engaged as a negotiation team member is subjected to the same stressors as other team members and, thus, can lose objectivity and the capacity to function independently as a clinical debriefer. Therefore, after a standoff has ended, it is recommended that a different clinical psychologist be brought in to conduct postincident debriefs of the team members (including the operational psychologist) and provide follow-on clinical services as needed.

Additional Considerations

Psychologists must always be mindful of the type of information utilized in a consultation and discern the relevance of the information to the task at hand. Despite being comfortable with certain sources of information as a psychologist, it is critical to view the overall impact of using certain data and records in the course of a consultation.

Use of Medical Records

Although the APA Ethics Code does not directly address the use of medical records in psychological consultation, the Report on Psychological Ethics and National Security (aka PENS Task Force Report: APA, 2005; see Appendix) advised against using an individual's medical record for interrogations in national security investigations and referenced Ethical Standard 3.04 (Avoiding Harm) and 3.08 (Exploitative Relationships). The broader issue of using medical records for indirect assessments has been addressed by Morgan et al. (2006), who noted that in general, medical and mental health records are of limited utility to psychological consultation in criminal, counterintelligence, or counterterrorism investigations.

However, there are times when medical and mental health records are beneficial to the negotiation process and can be helpful in bringing about a safe resolution to the conflict. In crisis negotiation situations, knowledge of the subject's medical and mental health history, triggers to stress and coping skills, and issues relevant to communication style empower the psychologist to better understand the subject, assess the subject's risk for violence, and consult with the negotiation team. Furthermore, medical records would provide information on the subject's current medications.

Consider a case in which a man took his family hostage using an explosive device strapped to his body. An interview with his brother revealed that the hostage taker suffered from diabetes. During the negotiation, his blood sugar began to climb and he required insulin. In an attempt to discern what medication he needed, his physician was contacted and his medical data revealed. One of the critical concerns was that as his conditioned worsened, so did his ability to process information and participate in the negotiation process. Thus, it was critical for the police to assist with keeping his diabetes stable to protect the hostages, the hostage taker, and the police surrounding the house.

The key to ethical crisis negotiation lies in emphasizing that the individual's medical record will not be used to his or her detriment but for the benefit of bringing a peaceful resolution to the situation. If the medical information would benefit the negotiation process, it should be used. However, the crisis negotiation team should not use medical information to exploit or manipulate the subject, and one of the roles of the consulting psychologist is to ensure that this does not occur. In addition, this constitutes an area of practice that demands prudence and one in which consulting psychologists must examine the ethical conflicts that may arise so that they are prepared to address them (Gottlieb, 1997, p. 266). If the crisis negotiation team decides to pursue access to the subject's medical and mental health records, the records should be obtained appropriately by the operational psychologist consulting to the negotiation team, handled with all the discretion used in clinical settings, and only sought when they are the sole source of available information that will ensure clarity and translate into actions that will promote safety and security for all involved (e.g. Grisso, 2003; Heilbrun, 2001).

Resolving Ethical Dilemmas Through Consultation

Psychologists consulting at crisis scenes may experience situations in which they face ethical dilemmas during the negotiation process and would benefit from consultation with other psychologists trained in crisis negotiations. The importance of seeking consultation is discussed in the Preamble of the APA Ethics Code: "The development of a dynamic set of ethical standards for psychologists' work-related conduct requires a personal commitment and lifelong effort to act ethically . . . and to consult with others concerning ethical problems" (APA, 2010). In order to reinforce this guideline, the PENS Task Force report advised, "Psychologists consult when they are facing ethical dilemmas" (APA, 2005, p.8). To facilitate the consultation process, psychologists should train together on past case studies, discuss ethical dilemmas, and keep a roster of trained experts who are available for urgent consultation needs.

DEVELOPING GUIDELINES FOR PSYCHOLOGISTS CONSULTING TO CRISIS NEGOTIATIONS

Developing guidelines for the psychologist who consults to crisis negotiators equates to developing clearly defined boundaries. Similar to any consultation in any operational setting, the psychologist must have a certain level of maturity and solid commitment to his or her role as a consultant to a strategic decision maker. Other authors (e.g., Morgan et al., 2006) have proposed guidelines for operational psychological consultation involved in indirect assessment for government agencies. In that spirit, the following guidelines are proposed for psychologists consulting in crisis negotiations.

Identify the Client, the Psychologist's Role, and the Roles of Other Team Members

The client is the law enforcement organization and its members. The members on scene include the scene commander, the negotiator, and the tactical squad (e.g., SWAT). The psychologist's role is to provide consultation without being unduly influenced by the emotionality of the event. The untrained psychologist in particular is at risk of stepping over his or her boundaries into other professional roles that compromise both the effectiveness and the value of the psychological consultation. It places the psychologist and the field of psychology in an ethical dilemma. The psychologist must think about what is being requested, be responsible when asked to do something that is inappropriate, and have a channel or chain of command in which to report and address such ethical violations.

Remain in the Role of an Expert Psychologist Consultant

A psychologist should never take on the role of a negotiator. The operational psychologist is more valuable to the team in the objective role of subject matter expert and loses that objectivity by taking over as a negotiator. It is critical that the psychologist identify the limitations of his or her role and not violate the boundaries of that role.

Remain Autonomous in Consultation and Free From External Influence and Pressure

The psychologist will likely experience influence and pressure from team members or leadership during the negotiation. Should this occur, the psychologist must focus on his or her assessment and not allow these entities to influence the consultation. It is easy for some of the most experienced operational psychologists to allow their consultative actions to be influenced by the high-energy environment and the agenda of on-scene officers and commanders. The psychologist should realize that police leadership is often under pressure from higher up professionals who may have a political agenda and who may be relatively uninformed of ground level operations.

Identify the Boundaries of the Psychologist's Role

The psychologist's role is to focus on the negotiation process and assist with bringing a peaceful resolution to the situation. The psychologist is not the on-site strategic decision maker. It is never the psychologist's role to make operational decisions, such as when to end the negotiation and enter the tactical phase. The psychologist's role is to inform and advise the strategic decision maker so that he or she can make the best informed decisions on resource allocation and course of action.

Appreciate the Uniqueness of Each Crisis Situation

Each case consultation requires careful thought and consideration. The context of the negotiation, the subject's mind-set, and the subject's risk for violence are dynamic and will change over time. Models and templates are not effectively applied across subjects. Similarly, the psychologist must address his or her own biases and prejudices and ensure that they not enter into the case consultation. Although past experience is helpful, the psychologist must appreciate that every case is unique.

Clearly Delineate the Boundaries Between Operational Consultants and Health Care Providers

The field of psychology has broadened enough that the profession should not expect a psychologist to go from therapy room to crisis scene. In general, a clinician is not well suited to handle the shift to operational consultation without first receiving the appropriate training, experience, and supervision. This is not to say that clinicians do not make good operational consultants. On the contrary, sound clinical skills are the foundation of operational consultation. However, it is critical that before a clinician serves in an operational role, he or she must first receive the appropriate training and supervision.

Establish and Maintain Professional Competence

Psychological consultation to crisis negotiations is a specialized discipline that requires intensive training with law enforcement negotiation teams and experienced crisis negotiation psychologists. This includes not just receiving crisis negotiation training but also acquiring the appropriate level of operational experience and supervision. Liaison with established crisis negotiation psychologists regarding the complex nature of crisis negotiation consultation is critical to resolving potential ethical dilemmas. Psychologists who are new to this field are advised to join their local crisis negotiation association, attend police and psychologist-specific trainings, liaise with other professional disciplines involved with crisis negotiations, and develop relationships with established crisis negotiation psychologists.

REFERENCES

American Psychological Association. (2010). *Ethical principles of psychologists and code of conduct (2002, Amended June 1, 2010)*. Retrieved from http://www.apa.org/ethics/code/index.aspx

American Psychological Association, Presidential Task Force on Psychological Ethics and National Security. (2005). *Report of the American Psychological Association Presidential Task Force on Psychological Ethics and National Security*. Retrieved April 20, 2008, from http://www.apa.org/releases/PENSTaskForceReportFinal.pdf

Borum, R., Fein, R., Vossekuil, B., & Burglund, J. (1999). Threat assessment: Defining an approach for evaluating risk of targeted violence. *Behavioral Sciences and the Law, 17*, 323–337. (Also available from http://www.secretservice.gov/ntac/ntac_bsl99.pdf)

Bush, S. S., & National Academy of Neuropsychology Policy and Planning Committee. (2005). Independent and court-ordered forensic neuropsychological examinations: Official statement of the National Academy of Neuropsychology. *Archives of Clinical Neuropsychology, 20*, 997–1007.

Fein, R. A., & Vossekuil, B. (1998). *Protective intelligence and threat assessment investigations* (NCJ Publication No. 170612). Washington, DC: U.S. Department of Justice.

Fowers, B. J. (2005). *Virtue and psychology: Pursuing excellence in ordinary practices*. Washington, DC: American Psychological Association.

Fuselier, G. D. (1981). A practical overview of hostage negotiations: Part 2. *FBI Law Enforcement Bulletin, 50*, 10–15.

Gelles, M. G. (1995). Psychological autopsy: An investigative aid. In M. Kurk & E. Scrivner (Eds.), *Police psychology in the 21st century* (pp. 337–355). New York: Erlbaum.

Gottleib, M. (1997). An ethics policy for family practice management. In R. Magee & D. Marsh (Eds.), *Ethical and legal issues in professional practice with families* (pp. 257–270). New York: Wiley.

Grisso, T. (2003). *Evaluating competencies: Forensic assessments and instruments* (2nd ed.). New York: Kluwer Academic/Plenum Publishers.

Handelsman, M. M., Knapp, S., & Gottlieb, M. C. (2002). Positive ethics. In C. R. Snyder & S. J. Lopez (Eds.), *Handbook of positive psychology* (pp. 731–744). New York: Oxford University Press.

Heilbrun, K. (2001). *Principles of forensic mental health assessment*. New York: Kluwer Academic/Plenum Publishers.

International Association of Chiefs of Police. (2006). *Guidelines for consulting police psychologists*. Retrieved April 20, 2008, from http://www.iacp.org/div_sec_com/sections/ConsultingPolicePsychologists.pdf

Knapp, S., Gottlieb, M. C., Berman, J., & Handelsman, M. M. (2007). When law and ethics collide: What should psychologists do? *Professional Psychology: Research and Practice, 38,* 54–59.

Manly, J. J., & Jacobs, D. M. (2002). Future directions in neuropsychological assessment with African Americans. In F. R. Ferraro (Ed.), *Minority and cross-cultural aspects of neuropsychological assessment* (pp. 79–96). Lisse, The Netherlands: Swets & Zeitliner.

McMains, M. J., & Mullins, W. C. (1996). *Crisis negotiations: Managing critical incidents and hostage situations in law enforcement and corrections.* Cincinnati, OH: Anderson Publishing.

Mohandie, K., & Meloy, J. R. (2000). Clinical and forensic indicators of "suicide by cop," *Journal of Forensic Sciences, 45,* 384–389.

Monahan, J. (1980). *Who is the client? The ethics of psychological intervention in the criminal justice system.* Washington, DC: American Psychological Association.

Morgan, C. A., Gelles, M. G., Steffian, G., Temporiani, H., Fortunati, F., Southwick, S., et al., (2006). Consulting to government agencies—Indirect assessments. *Psychiatry, 3,* 24–28.

Patai, R. (2007). *The Arab mind.* Long Island City, NY: Hatherleigh.

Post, J. (2004) *Leaders and their followers in a dangerous world: The psychology of political behavior.* Ithaca, NY: Cornell University Press.

Rowe, K. L., Gelles, M. G., & Palarea, R. E. (2006). Crisis and hostage negotiation. In C. H. Kennedy & E. A. Zillmer (Eds.), *Military psychology: Clinical and operational applications.* New York: Guilford Press.

Schreiber, M. (1973). *An after action report of terrorist activities, 20th Olympic games, Munich, West Germany.* Unpublished manuscript.

Schlossberg, H. (1979). Police response to hostage situations. In J. T. O'Brien & M. Marcus (Eds.), *Crime and justice in America.* New York: Pergamon Press.

Williams, T. J., Picano, J. J., Roland, R. R., & Banks, L. M. (2006). Introduction to operational psychology. In C. H. Kennedy & E. A. Zillmer (Eds.), *Military psychology: Clinical and operational applications* (pp. 193–214). New York: Guilford Press.

7

OPERATIONAL PSYCHOLOGY: PROACTIVE ETHICS IN A CHALLENGING WORLD

THOMAS J. WILLIAMS AND CARRIE H. KENNEDY

The chapters in this volume provide the basis for an ethical foundation and framework for the various roles and responsibilities of operational psychologists. It is evident that operational psychologists experience special demands and bear social responsibilities in providing services in difficult and demanding nontraditional settings. Therefore, psychologists must find a way, as did the founding members of the profession, to reconcile the science, practice, law, and ethics with national security threats posed by avowed enemies of our way of life (Yerkes, 1918).

A code of ethics cannot anticipate all the ethical concerns that psychologists may face and reflects the reality that practical issues may arise that result in a conflict between the law and ethics (Knapp & VandeCreek, 2003, 2006). Indeed, the American Psychological Association's "Ethical Principles of Psychologists and Code of Conduct" (APA Ethics Code; APA, 2010a) anticipates this conflict. Standard 1.02, Conflicts Between Ethics and Law, Regulations, or Other Governing Legal Authority, which was amended

The views expressed in this article are those of the authors and do not reflect the official policy or position of the U.S. Department of the Army, U.S. Department of the Navy, U.S. Department of Defense, or the U.S. government.

effective June 1, 2010, by a resolution of the APA Council of Representatives (APA, 2010b) states,

> If psychologists' ethical responsibilities conflict with law, regulations, or other governing legal authority, psychologists clarify the nature of the conflict, make known their commitment to the Ethics Code and take steps to resolve the conflict consistent with the General Principles and Ethical Standards of the Ethics Code. Under no circumstances may this standard be used to justify or defend violating human rights. (APA, 2010a)

This revision significantly alters the responsibility of a psychologist who finds him- or herself in this conflict by removing the stipulation that a psychologist "*may* adhere to the requirements of the law" (emphasis added) even though the code never mandated a "must" adhere to the law, regulations, or other government authority. Since it is generally accepted that society steps in with laws to protect the interests of its citizens, it seems important to carefully consider the potential risk of misplaced deliberations that are based on an individual's perception for how his or her professional ethical responsibility conflicts with that greater societal interest. Certainly, there must exist some deliberative process to ensure no one within a profession views his or her own actions as above the law by cloaking those actions within an ethical framework that the profession sanctions, potentially causing an ethics code to serve as a de facto second-order legal system. With emerging practice areas such as operational psychology, we hope the wisdom gained from efforts to reconcile these conflicts serves both the interest of the profession and the greater good of the society we seek to promote.

Toward that end, psychologists who find themselves providing services in new areas of practice have a responsibility to remain sensitive to potential ethical conflicts (see, e.g., Howe, 2003) and to apply their professional judgment and ethical decision-making skills to resolve any conflicts as they arise. The collective chapters of this volume provide recognition by operational psychologists of that responsibility.

In the support they provide to U.S. national security programs and services, operational psychologists often find themselves working in very austere and challenging cross-cultural settings around the world. The ethical standards of the APA Ethics Code appear to apply more squarely to traditional health care settings and traditional clinical services and less clearly to national security and law enforcement arenas in which organizational and legal demands often conflict with the Ethics Code (cf. Knapp & VandeCreek, 2003). The diverse settings and myriad situations around the world in which operational psychologists may find themselves offer particular challenges (see, e.g., Shumate & Borum, 2006; Staal & King, 2000; Staal & Stephenson, 2006; Stephenson & Staal, 2007). Although these challenging situations must be weighed against the five general principles of the APA Ethics Code (2010a—Principle A: Beneficence and Nonmaleficence, Principle B: Fidelity and Responsibility, Principle C: Integrity, Principle D: Justice, and Principle E: Respect for People's Rights and Dignity—no ethics code could be expected to provide all the guidance or answer all the questions that might arise. Nor should it try to do so.

Although framed within a clinical context, the ethics of operational psychology must provide an "active, deliberative, and creative approach" for confronting in a practical manner an almost unimaginable diversity of situations, each with its own shifting questions, demands, and responsibilities to "prompt, guide, and inform our ethical considerations" (Pope & Vasquez, 1998, p. 17). Given the number of publications focused on ethics for traditional clinical practice, it should come as no surprise that operational psychology, as a new and emerging area of practice, may face even greater challenges in defining ethical practice (Williams, Picano, Roland, & Banks, 2006).

Similar to other psychologists, operational psychologists are likely to

> encounter ethical dilemmas for which a clear ethical response is elusive . . . by situations whose meaning varies sharply depending on the context in which it is viewed, by limits in the degree to which science is currently able to understand certain conditions . . . [and operational psychologists] must be prepared to examine these dilemmas actively as a normal, expected part of their work. (Pope & Vasquez, 1998, p. 18)

This statement acknowledges the challenges that operational psychologists face, perhaps to a greater extent than other psychologists, in reconciling their ethical deliberations with the practical realities and dynamic nature of their duties.

It is worth noting that a primary reason for the promulgation of an ethics code along with enforceable sanctions for a profession is both to gain and maintain the trust of the public and society served by that profession (Koocher & Keith-Spiegel, 1998). Consequently, the Ethics Code has remained responsive to and provides an ongoing awareness of the fact that psychologists often confront novel situations that call into question old practices (Jeffrey, Rankin, & Jeffrey, 1992). A profession that does not recognize the dynamic forces that help to shape its applications is certain to lose its relevancy over time. The impetus for this book is this inherent inner tension between traditional practices and new ethical challenges. Although there has long been recognition for the need to balance ethical practice against organizational demands, recent efforts to limit the settings within which operational psychologists can provide their services add another dimension for the profession (see, e.g., Carter & Abeles, 2009).

As the chapters contained in this volume reveal, operational psychologists, like others in emerging disciplines before them, have been careful to recognize and to seek guidance for their professional activities. They remain attuned to

Principle A: Beneficence and Nonmaleficence, ensuring by their actions the need to "strive to benefit those with whom they work and take care to do no harm" (APA, 2010a). Needless to say, issues arise that confront operational psychologists with a changing landscape of political, organizational, and social demands for their support in new, applied settings, and they are obligated to respond in an appropriate manner as demanded by APA's Ethics Code. As is revealed throughout these chapters, psychologists involved in these roles quickly recognized how their "scientific and professional judgments and actions may affect the lives of others [and reinforced their need to remain] . . . alert to and guard against personal, financial, social, organizational, or political factors that might lead to misuse of their influence" (APA, 2010a).

OPERATIONAL PSYCHOLOGY: RESPONSIVE AND RELEVANT

Psychology as a profession must remain responsive and relevant not only to the opportunities that promote societal welfare but also to the challenges that pose a threat to that welfare. It is fair to say that many more psychologists are comfortable with the health care provider and other traditional roles than they are with operational roles. For example, many authors who address ethical issues for psychologists help shape that impression by emphasizing clinical health care setting roles. They note that "psychologists, like all health care professionals" recognize that psychology is also "an academic and research discipline" (Knapp & VandeCreek, 2006, p. 5). Indeed, the Ethics Code uses a principle-based ethics commonly used for biomedical ethics and framed within the context of and designed to address patient–provider issues (Beauchamp & Childress, 2001). This aspect of the Ethics Code recognizes psychologists as moral agents (cf. London, 1986), with the code guiding, though not in absolute terms, their behavior and actions, which most often are framed within the context of ensuring good health care delivery. Given this biomedical bias, it is easy to understand why some within the profession may find discomfort in certain issues or actions by psychologists acting in less traditional and more nonmedical roles (e.g., operational). It also helps psychologists to understand why attempts are made to frame these roles within the context of a professional and presumptive treatment relationship with a patient and the rights that pertain to the patient. Even within the latter context, there is recognition that psychologists are likely to encounter circumstances that may offend the personal and professional ethics of other psychologists (Knapp & Vandecreek, 2006). Indeed, a survey of senior-level psychologists revealed that a majority acknowledged they had intentionally broken the law or violated a formal ethical standard out of consideration for "client welfare or another value" (Pope & Bajt, 1988, p. 828).

In many ways, it is this tension between the tendency to view all psychology activities as patient health care oriented and the reality of their duties that often confronts applied operational providers. When the actions of operational psychologists are viewed purely within a biomedical model frame of reference, the full spectrum of legal and administratively important operational activities cannot be considered. Taking this stance also increases the risk of leaving psychologists vulnerable to a conceptual breach between those ethical guidelines that should guide professional behavior and their often unique practice settings and challenges around the world. Consequently, it is important for operational psychologists to increase their understanding and awareness of how to constructively and proactively use the Ethics Code in establishing guiding principles and parameters for ethical practice within the context of operational activities. The chapters within this volume are intended to address these important issues.

OPERATIONAL PSYCHOLOGY: HISTORICAL FOUNDATIONS AND CURRENT ISSUES

Psychologists have frequently expanded their roles into the areas of public policy and political process during threats to national security. For example, Reiff (1971) provided a review of how behavioral scientists may increase their political and public policy roles during wartime or when there is a perceived threat to the well-being of society, and Kamin (1974) reviewed the early political involvement and influence of several esteemed psychologists in support of national defense. More recently, and in a different but related context, DeLeon et al. (1996) called for psychologists to proactively embrace opportunities to "focus on society's needs" and to share their expertise to help create public policy, recognize the increasing opportunities open to psychologists, and remove the "self-imposed barriers" that have served to block a broader vision of psychology that includes "science, practice, education, and public interest." Is there a greater public interest than to help preserve the national security that affords and preserves the freedom to pursue science, practice, and education?

How then can psychologists help to bridge this gap between the public interest of protecting life, liberty, and families? Operational psychologists must seek to use the full spectrum of psychological expertise without compromising professional and personal ethics that form the expression of their underlying values. In essence, they must provide their services in an ethical manner as they confront the challenges to the values of the United States as a nation and a people, using the model developed by the early leaders of the profession of psychology to help guide their actions.

American psychology has a long tradition of providing support to the nation in time of peril (see, e.g., Boring, 1945; Kennedy & McNeil, 2006; McGuire, 1990; Yerkes, 1918). Yerkes (1918) noted how psychology as a profession "brought to the front the desirability and the possibility of dealing scientifically and effectively with the principal human factors in military organization and activit[ies]" (p. 114). He convened a group of prominent psychologists to see "what, if anything, could psychology offer the country to support the war effort?" and concluded that "selection, training, aviation, and motivation [problems related to military service]" were viable (Driskell & Olmstead, 1989, p. 43). Yerkes (1918) was among the first psychologists to note the personal and professional satisfaction from having made a contribution to the nation's military:

> Finally, it remains for me to say that from the very start there has been conspicuous enthusiasm for psychological military service and loyalty in the service. The work has been arduous, the discouragements often numerous and serious but in spite of them our various lines of work have been carried forward satisfactorily and in most instances with surprising rapidity. Everyone who has had opportunity to share in the work obviously feels that he has contributed to our military progress and has rendered more substantial service through the application of his professional training than would have been possible in any other line. (pp. 114–15)

During World War II, seven practical uses of psychology were identified as of immediate relevance to the military. These included observation (i.e., sensory perception), occupational performance, selection and classification, training, personal adjustment to military life, social relations (e.g., cultural competency and leadership), and psychological warfare (Boring, 1945). More recently, an APA president asked the military, "Tell me how you can use me!" (DeLeon et al., 1996, p. 436).

This nation has become increasingly aware that political and military conflict is not necessarily just between nations with specific geographical boundaries. Americans have known for some time about the increasing threat posed by small groups of extremists who may represent a small percentage of the population of several countries. President Clinton's administration was among the first to recognize the threat posed by transnational terrorist organizations, noting:

> The variety of sub-state and supra-state actors that affect the security environment will continue to grow in number and capability. Violent, religiously-motivated terrorist organizations have eclipsed more traditional, politically-motivated movements. The latter often refrained from mass casualty operations for fear of alienating their constituencies and actors who could advance their agendas or for the lack of material and technical

skill. Religious zealots rarely exhibit such restraint and actively seek to maximize carnage. . . . Over the next 15 years, terrorists will become even more sophisticated in their targeting, propaganda, and political action operations. Terrorist state sponsors like Iran will continue to provide vital support to a disparate mix of terrorist groups and movements. (U.S. Department of Defense, 1998, p. 79)

The bombings of the U.S. embassy in Kenya, the attack on the USS Cole, and the Al Qaeda attacks on September 11, 2001, served as powerful and unsettling reminders of the unconventional nature of emerging political conflicts and how important it is to attend to the individual behaviors of terrorist organization members (cf. Mickolus, 2002). Psychologists need to ask "in what various ways, military and nonmilitary, can we, as psychologists, help to make the world safe, secure, and just?" In Yerkes's day, the enemy was more conventional and easier to identify. It was therefore also easier to justify the involvement of psychologists in the military, although even then many of the more academically focused psychologists opposed any involvement. Today's enemy of world peace is more elusive, and the challenges of intelligence gathering and military defense as well as worldwide economic development and improved quality of life for all are more complex than ever. Psychologists with behavioral and psychological expertise are needed in operational psychology as well as in other areas affected by rapid social change to preserve freedom for all, safety, and social and economic well-being.

In a manner similar to psychologists' professional forbears (see, e.g., Office of Strategic Studies, 1948; Reiff, 1971), today's operational psychologists have recognized the "new reality" and are responding to requests for their psychological expertise to help counter the threat posed to the well-being of American society and the world by those who have vowed to destroy the American way of life.

Many of the issues addressed in this volume reflect efforts to balance the competition between individual interests and societal interests and make known the ethical conflicts. The chapters also reflect an effort to demonstrate a commitment to an all-important function of the Ethics Code for the psychology profession: that psychologists respect the dignity and rights of individuals and that operational psychologists provide and promote an ethical practice in support of a vast array of clinical and nonclinical services, information, support, or interventions. As Blickle (2004) noted, the professional and ethics code should not attempt to function as an instrument to somehow "legislate" a better the world; that is not an appropriate role. Rather, psychologists' code of professional behavior should define good rules of practice, guiding professionals in the types of behaviors and actions that will promote and "create public trust and confidence in the profession and its members" (Blickle, 2004, p. 273). As such, there must also be established procedures for monitoring and observing the actions of those within the profession along with sanctioning mechanisms for those who deviate from the accepted standards. As the profession increasingly pushes to become more culturally sensitive (see, e.g., Pettifor, 2004), we must accept that many of the "cultures in which psychologists are active may have varying moral standards" (Blickle, 2004, p. 273). As we hope is evident from the various contributions contained within this volume, operational psychologists have diligently adhered to the value base of the profession of psychology: "rationality, empirical support for assertions, impartiality, openness to revisions, and acknowledgement of the limits to one's own competence" (Blickle, 2004, p. 274).

Expanding the Roles of Psychologists Into Operational Areas

The nontraditional roles of operational psychologists as practiced in a variety of settings along with consideration of the ethical issues posed by these expanding roles are the focus of this book. As the profession of psychology has expanded its roles and services and as issues have arisen and a consensus has begun to be built about the propriety of psychologists assuming these roles, the APA Ethics Code has expanded to address those recognized roles. The timing and sequence of these changes is important: Historically, as the roles and scope of practice have expanded, so too has the Ethics Code in response. Accordingly, the Ethics Code can serve as a rational foundation for how the profession of psychology should act in remaining responsive and relevant to a changing world by providing "a common set of principles and standards upon which psychologists build their professional and scientific work" (APA, 2010a). Nonetheless, as with shifting paradigms of practice (Kuhn, 1970), expanding roles and areas of practice among psychologists are always the subject of much debate, prompting the need to expand the Ethics Code as the new domains result in increasing numbers of ethical dilemmas (Kennedy & Moore, 2008).

Clinical psychology practice and the focus on mental health have helped to shape psychology's professional identity and have played a critical role in the development of the profession. The general principles in the Ethics Code have health care ethics as their common ethical foundation (Beaucamp & Childress, 2001). However, a number of prominent psychologists and leaders within the profession have persuasively argued that the profession of psychology should not have as its end goal the further refinement of a professional identity that is too focused on health care delivery (Resnick, DeLeon, & VandenBos, 1997). As some have noted, if psychologists are to have a maturing profession with a more expansive future, then "psychology needs to get out of the same self-imposed ruts and broaden its horizon" (DeLeon et al., 1996). In the spirit of Yerkes and other psychologists at the turn of the last century, operational psychologists offer a valued and broadened horizon for the profession.

Policy and Politics

There have been calls for psychology and psychologists to consider their roles and responsibilities by taking a broader public policy perspective on how they can use their expertise (DeLeon, Bennett, & Bricklin, 1997). Failing to heed this advice may significantly weaken the profession of psychology because the policy formation process moves on whether psychologists are part of it or not. As society and the context for services change, psychologists are either shaped by these forces in a manner that others perceive as important or psychologists take on the role of helping shape these forces in a manner guided by the blending of science, education, reason, and the practical dictates of the situation. In a dynamic and evolving policy domain, efforts to frame an ethical practice of psychology in response to proposed policy changes have often resulted in unintended gaps in the newly revised policy and/or practice, and then the process starts anew. As addressed earlier, when the profession remains responsive to these forces rather than eschewing them, psychologists continue to remain relevant to the society that benefits from their action. The subfield of forensic psychology offers a very good model for the development of standards of practice that are uniquely applicable to the new area of practice (e.g., Perrin & Sales, 1994). Table 7.1 provides a model for operational psychology ethical decision-making that is adapted from Bush, Connell, and Denney (2006).

The Future of Operational Psychology: Policy, Practice, and Ethics

The authors of this volume examine the various roles operational psychologists play and the likely ethical dilemmas they will encounter. It is interesting to note that one of the criticisms directed at the applications of operational psychology is that it does not have an empirical base for its practice. This is made more interesting when juxtaposed against the fact that a majority of clinical settings do not provide evidence-based practice (Addis & Krasnow, 2000; Levant, 2005), and controversies remain about evidence-based practice and empirically supported treatments in more traditional clinical practice (see, e.g., Kendall & Beidas, 2007). This is not uncommon because "scientific advances in treatment are usually not implemented in the health care system for 20–25 years" (Hogan, 2003, cited in Kendall & Beidas, 2007). This representation is offered not to obviate the need for operational psychologists to remain guided by and informed about sound research. Rather, it is offered in the spirit of muting criticism sometimes directed toward operational psychology and promoting in its place the same "collaborative and collegial exchange between two perspectives" of research and practice (cf. Kendall & Beidas, 2007).

TABLE 7.1
Framework for Operational Psychology Ethical Decision Making

Professional activities/Context	Decision-making steps
Identify the operational psychology roles, activities, and responsibilities	1. Legal purpose 2. Medical purpose 3. Type of expertise most needed 4. Competence 5. Context and setting
Relevant ethical issues	1. Ethical issues 2. Nature of access: direct versus indirect assessment 3. Benefit to society versus benefit to individual 4. As complexity increases, so does need for consultation
Applicable laws, regulations, and authorities	1. Legal rights of individual 2. Protection of society 3. Access to legal authorities 4. Course of action consistent with Ethics Code 5. Professional organization foundation for actions 6. Relevant laws, research and/or publications (e.g., international law, Geneva Conventions)
Cultural issues and settings	1. Linguistic and cultural differences 2. Environmental cues and intent 3. Cognitive and behavioral style of relating 4. Cultural divergence versus convergence 5. Examination of own personal beliefs and values 6. Potential positive and negative consequences of actions (e.g., losing face) 7. Use of third-party observers 8. Social psychology of interaction 9. Collateral sources or contacts
Consultation	1. Peer review or consultation 2. Calibration of understanding of issues 3. Clear representation of findings
Possible courses of action or solutions	1. Weighing ethical principles 2. Deliberation on possible solutions

Note. Adapted from *Ethical Practice in Forensic Psychology: A Systematic Model for Decision Making* (pp. 27–35), by S. S. Bush, M. A. Connell, and R. L. Denney, 2006, Washington, DC: American Psychological Association. Copyright 2006 by the American Psychological Association.

Toward that end, operational psychologists need to ensure they maintain a *science of psychology* base to all of their actions. Only then can they ensure a shared and respected knowledge from which to assess and understand human behavior so as to solve complex problems. Operational psychology, perhaps more than any specialty area, requires the practitioner to strive for expertise across several areas of specialization within the psychological and social sciences literature (e.g., clinical psychology, social and personality, sensation and perception, learning, cross-cultural, political psychology, leadership, national defense policy, Geneva Convention and Human Rights, to name but a few). A framework for identifying a number of potential areas for future growth and research is provided below.

- Identification and specification of settings and roles specific to operational psychology as opposed to applied clinical psychology. In what contexts and settings do the two differ?
- Military psychologists in most cases are designated as medical health care providers and as such are considered *noncombatants* under the Geneva Convention. However, operational psychologists in most cases are not providing health care. Therefore, can and should operational psychologists possess Geneva Convention protection as health care providers or by their actions do they lose that status? Is that status job-specific or does it relate to the person such that he or she can move in and out of that status?
- Identification and validation of practice guidelines for use in establishing levels of competency and potential for board certification recognition. What experiences and level of training are required for practice?
- Psychology of interrogation support: observations and lessons learned by psychologists in support of these roles. How do psychologists capture the important contributions and lessons learned?
- Differential determinations of the cultural and language influences relevant to understanding the motivations and behaviors of insurgents, terrorists, and combatants. What have psychologists learned so far?
- The relevance of cross-cultural differences and influences when defining ethical practice for psychologists in the service of society (the greater good) rather than individual interests. How do psychologists balance the differing morals and values of other societies against an Ethics Code based on what psychologists value in American society?

The Ethics Code has been revised nine times since its first version in direct response to changes in the practices and roles of psychologists. In the cases of some fields, standards have been developed that are uniquely applicable to those fields (e.g., research, forensics; Perrin & Sales, 1994).

In many ways, the various issues and problems addressed in this chapter and throughout this volume share a common core and are, in part, in line with rapid social and technological changes increasingly recognized as the 21st century's ethical challenges for psychology (Koocher, 2007). How do psychologists balance the beneficence and nonmaleficence along with fidelity and responsibility that serve as the foundation for the Ethics Code (APA, 2010a) with professional, scientific, and personal responsibilities to the society in which psychologists live and to the increasingly global community? As Koocher (2007) related, both history and law have long recognized that psychologists have an obligation to carefully weigh the role of "healer" against the obligation to "the greater good of society" (p. 379). Psychologists must face "the fact that some of our professional duties may force us [to] choose to take actions potentially harmful to an individual client but deemed beneficial to society as a whole" (Koocher, 2007, p. 379). Granted, this is no easily resolvable dilemma and often causes psychologists to try to reconcile their personal, professional, and societal obligations. Following Stone (1984), who stated that "justice is itself a beneficence" and through their professional actions, psychologists must balance between "a beneficence to a society of unidentified persons" (i.e., a general good) and the "practical ethical duty" to those to whom they provide their services.

As psychologists increasingly find themselves drawn into situations with a multitude of "social and political interests . . . across hierarchies of individuals to whom we owe various degrees of professional ethics" (Koocher, 2007, p. 381), three considerations (see Table 7.2) help guide and establish an ethical framework. This framework offers a succinct but highly useful ethical role management strategy for operational psychologists as they consider their professional roles and responsibilities in various settings.

CONCLUSION

As noted earlier, the intent for this volume is to help establish the ethical framework for the emerging subdiscipline of operational psychology. As the contributions attest, the field is rich with opportunity, and its success has been

TABLE 7.2
Recommendations for Ethical Role Management

Roles	Management
Clarify professional and personal obligations at outset of professional relationship	1. Organizational versus personal 2. Other parties 3. Reduce risk of confusion
Carefully weigh legal and ethical standards with emergent need	1. One individual's need over society's need 2. Professional obligation versus personal, political consideration (i.e., apolitical) 3. Public policy decision-making process
Professional duty	1. Consider welfare and best interests of most vulnerable party in chain of individuals to whom duty is owed 2. Identify opportunities to optimize outcome 3. Determine if vulnerable party is the public at large

Note. Adapted from "Twenty-First Century Ethical Challenges for Psychology" by G. P. Koocher, 2007, American Psychologist, 62, p. 381. Copyright 2007 by the American Psychological Association.

attributable largely to the value-added expertise and clarity with which military, U.S. Department of Defense, and other government agency psychologists have carried their professional and scientific abilities toward the changing nature of the forces of political conflict in the world today.

As psychologists have explored the challenges and the practice associated with the expression of these professional abilities, it has become clear that the APA Ethics Code requires a broader consideration of the various settings within which the practice of operational psychology may occur. For example, psychologists must carefully consider the various roles, cultural settings, policies, and full implications of attempting to view of practice of psychology in settings around the world. In addition, psychologists must allow themselves to consider when the aspirational goal of beneficence carries more weight toward the society than to the specific individual. The attacks of September 11, 2001, were largely motivated by a group of extremists intent on destroying Americans' way of life. If psychologists view their actions as individuals, they are terrorists, but if psychologists view their larger true intent, they are genocidists. Through the cultural lens of "individualistic" rights that serves as the foundation for the APA Ethics Code, a code that is promulgated from psychologists' medically based, patient-oriented system, paradoxically, psychologists' first duty would be to the terrorist, with the assumption that doing so promotes a common good. Unfortunately, that is not always the case. Therefore, and importantly, any changes to the APA Ethics Code should reflect both the practical realities of a changing world in which not only operational psychologists but all psychologists provide their services. Psychologists also should avoid any politically motivated changes to the Ethics Code that could serve as a tool to restrict activities without considering the full legal, scientific, and practical realities of that change for both the profession and society.

Psychologists working for national security organizations are finding themselves increasingly sought after to fill these nontraditional psychology roles. As operational psychologists rise to meet these challenges and opportunities by leveraging their expertise, there is a sound ethical foundation for these activities. And perhaps just as important, operational psychologists are making these contributions with the same sense of obligation and readiness that many of the early members of APA shared:

> In the present situation, it is obviously desirable that the psychologists of the country act unitedly in the interests of defense. Our knowledge and our methods are of importance to the military service of our country, and it is our duty to cooperate to the fullest extent and immediately toward the increased efficiency of our Army and Navy. Formalities are not in order. We should act at once as a professional group as well as individually. (Yerkes, 1918, p. 86)

REFERENCES

Addis, M., & Krasnow, A. (2000). A national survey of practicing psychologists' attitudes toward psychotherapy treatment manuals. *Journal of Consulting and Clinical Psychology, 68,* 331–339.

American Psychological Association. (2010a). *Ethical principles of psychologists and code of conduct (2002, Amended June 1, 2010).* Retrieved from http://www.apa. org/ethics/code/index.aspx.

American Psychological Association. (2010b). Report of the ethics committee, 2009. *American Psychologist.* Advance online publication. doi:10.1037/a0019515.

Beauchamp, T., & Childress, J. (2001). *Principles of biomedical ethics* (5th ed.). New York: Oxford University Press.

Blickle, G. (2004). Commentaries on "Professional ethics across national boundaries" by Jean L. Pettifor: Professional ethics needs a theoretical background. *European Psychologist, 9,* 273–274.

Boring, E. G. (Ed.). (1945). *Psychology for the Armed Services.* Oxford, England: Infantry Journal.

Bush, S. S., Connell, M. A., & Denney, R. L. (2006). *Ethical practice in forensic psychology: A systematic model for decision making.* Washington, DC: American Psychological Association.

Carter, L. A., & Abeles, N. (2009). Ethics, prisoner interrogation, national security, and the media. *Psychological Science, 6,* 11–21.

DeLeon, P. H., Bennett, B. E., & Bricklin, P. M. (1997). Ethics and public policy formulation: A case example related to prescription privileges. *Professional Psychology: Research and Practice, 28,* 518–525.

DeLeon, P. H., Howell, W. C., Newman, R., Brown, A. B., Keita, G. P., & Sexton, J. L. (1996). Expanding roles in the twenty-first century. In R. J. Resnick & R. H. Rozensky (Eds.), *Health psychology through the life span: Practice and research opportunities* (pp. 427–453). Washington, DC: American Psychological Association.

Driskell, J. E., & Olmstead, B. (1989). Psychology and the military: Research applications and trends. *American Psychologist, 44,* 43–54.

Hogan, M. (2003). The president's new freedom commission: Recommendations to transform mental health care in America. *Psychiatric Services, 54,* 1467–1474.

Howe, E. G. (2003). Dilemmas in military medical ethics since 9/11. *Kennedy Institute of Ethics Journal, 13,* 175–188.

Jeffrey, T. B., Rankin, R. J., & Jeffrey, L. K. (1992). In service of two masters: The ethical–legal dilemma faced by military psychologists. *Professional Psychology: Research and Practice, 23,* 91–95.

Kamin, L. J. (1974). *The science and politics of I.Q.* Potomac, MD: Erlbaum.

Kendall, P. C., & Beidas, R. S. (2007). Smoothing the trail for dissemination of evidence-based practices for youth: Flexibility within fidelity. *Professional Psychology: Research and Practice, 38,* 13–20.

Kennedy, C. H., & McNeil, J. A. (2006). A history of military psychology. In C. H. Kennedy & E. A. Zillmer (Eds.), *Military psychology: Clinical and operational applications*. New York: Guilford Press.

Kennedy, C. H., & Moore, B. A. (2008). Evolution of clinical military psychology ethics. *Military Psychology, 20*, 1–6.

Knapp, S. J., & VandeCreek, L. D. (2003). *A guide to the 2002 revision of the APA Ethics Code*. Sarsota, FL: Professional Resource Press.

Knapp, S. J., & VandeCreek, L. D. (2006). *Practical ethics for psychologists: A positive approach*. Washington, DC: American Psychological Association.

Koocher, G. P. (2007). Twenty-first century ethical challenges for psychology. *American Psychologist, 62*, 375–384.

Koocher, G. P., & Keith-Spiegel, P. (1998) *Ethics in psychology: Professional standards and cases*. New York: Oxford University Press.

Kuhn, T. S. (1970). *The structure of scientific revolutions*. (2nd ed.). Chicago: University of Chicago Press.

Levant, R. F. (2005). *Report of the 2005 Presidential Task Force on Evidence-Based Practice*. Retrieved June 29, 2008, from http://www.apa.org/practice/ebpreport.pdf

London, P. (1986). *The modes and morals of psychotherapy* (2nd ed.). New York: Harper & Row.

McGuire, F. L. (1990). *Psychology aweigh! A history of clinical psychology in the United States Navy, 1900–1988*. Washington, D.C.: American Psychological Association.

Mickolus, E. E. (2002). How do we know we're winning the war against terrorists? Issues in measurement. *Studies in Conflict & Terrorism, 25*, 151–160.

Office of Strategic Services. (1948). *Assessment of men: Selection of personnel for the Office of Strategic Services*. New York: Rinehart.

Perrin, G. I., & Sales, B. D. (1994). Forensic standards in the American Psychological Association's new ethics code. *Professional Psychology: Research and Practice, 25*, 376–381.

Pettifor, J. L. (2004). Professional ethics across national boundaries. *European Psychologist, 9*, 264–272.

Pope, K. S., & Bajt, T. R. (1988). When laws and values conflict: A dilemma for psychologists. *American Psychologist, 43*, 828–829.

Pope, K. S., & Vasquez, M. J. T. (1998). *Ethics in psychotherapy and counseling: A practical guide* (2nd ed.). San Francisco: Jossey-Bass.

Reiff, R. R. (1971) Community psychology and public policy. In J. C. Glidewell & G. Rosenblum (Eds.), *Issues in community psychology and preventive mental health* (pp. 33–54). New York: Behavioral Publications.

Resnick, R. J., DeLeon, P. H., & VandenBos, G. R. (1997). Evolution of professional issues in psychology: Training standards, legislative recognition, and boundaries of practice. In J. R. Matthews & C. E. Walker (Eds.), *Basic skills and professional issues in clinical psychology* (pp. 281–303). Needham Heights, MA: Allyn & Bacon.

Shumate, S., & Borum, R. (2006). Psychological support to defense counterintelligence operations. *Military Psychology*, *18*, 283–296.

Staal, M. A., & King, R. E. (2000). Managing a multiple relationship environment: The ethics of military psychology. *Professional Psychology: Research and Practice*, *31*, 698–705.

Staal, M. A., & Stephenson, J. A. (2006). Operational psychology: An emerging subdiscipline. *Military Psychology*, *18*, 269–282.

Stephenson, J. A., & Staal, M. A. (2007). Operational psychology: What constitutes expertise? *The Specialist*, *26*, 13, 30–31.

Stone, A. A. (1984). The ethical boundaries of forensic psychiatry: A view from the ivory tower. *Bulletin of the American Academy of Psychiatry and Law*, *12*, 209–219.

U.S. Department of Defense. (1998). *William S. Cohen, Report of the Secretary of Defense to the President and Congress*. Washington, DC: U.S. Government Printing Office. Available at http://www.dod.mil/execsec/adr98/chap1.html

Williams, T. J., Picano, J. J., Roland, R. R., & Banks, L. M. (2006). Introduction to operational psychology. In C. H. Kennedy & E. A. Zillmer (Eds.). *Military psychology: Clinical and operational applications* (pp. 193–214). New York: Guilford Press.

Yerkes, R. M. (1918). Psychology in relation to war. *Psychological Review*, *25*, 85–115.

APPENDIX: THE TWELVE GUIDING STATEMENTS OF THE APA PRESIDENTIAL TASK FORCE ON PSYCHOLOGICAL ETHICS AND NATIONAL SECURITY (APA, 2005).[1]

1. Psychologists do not engage in, direct, support, facilitate, or offer training in torture or other cruel, inhuman, or degrading treatment.
2. Psychologists are alert to acts of torture and other cruel, inhuman, or degrading treatment and have an ethical responsibility to report these acts to the appropriate authorities.
3. Psychologists who serve in the role of supporting an interrogation do not use health care related information from an individual's medical record to the detriment of the individual's safety and well-being.
4. Psychologists do not engage in behaviors that violate the laws of the United States, although psychologists may refuse for ethical reasons to follow laws or orders that are unjust or that violate basic principles of human rights.
5. Psychologists are aware of and clarify their role in situations where the nature of their professional identity and professional function may be ambiguous.
6. Psychologists are sensitive to the problems inherent in mixing potentially inconsistent roles such as health care provider and consultant to an interrogation, and refrain from engaging in such multiple relationships.
7. Psychologists may serve in various national security-related roles, such as a consultant to an interrogation, in a manner that is consistent with the Ethics Code, and when doing so psychologists are mindful of factors unique to these roles and contexts that require special ethical consideration.
8. Psychologists who consult on interrogation techniques are mindful that the individual being interrogated may not have

---

[1]American Psychological Association, Presidential Task Force on Psychological Ethics and National Security. (2005, June). *Report of the American Psychological Association Presidential Task Force on Psychological Ethics and National Security*. Retrieved March 10, 2005, from http://www.apa.org/releases/PENSTaskForceReportFinal.pdf

engaged in untoward behavior and may not have information of interest to the interrogator.

9. Psychologists make clear the limits of confidentiality.

10. Psychologists are aware of and do not act beyond their competencies, except in unusual circumstances, such as set forth in the Ethics Code.

11. Psychologists clarify for themselves the identity of their client and retain ethical obligations to individuals who are not their clients.

12. Psychologists consult when they are facing difficult ethical dilemmas.

INDEX

Behavioral Science Consultation Teams
(BSCTs), 11, 94–100
Behavioral scientists, 129
Behnke, S., 87, 89
Beidas, R. S., 133
Beneficence, 30, 61, 87, 128, 135, 136
Bias
in assessment and selection, 42, 45
biomedical, 128
Blickel, G., 132
Board certification, 17
Boltz, Frank, 107, 108
Boundaries, of psychologist roles, 120
Boundary violations, 118
Breaches of trust, 8
BSCs. *See* Behavioral Science
Consultants
BSCTs. *See* Behavioral Science
Consultation Teams

California Court of Appeals, 34
California Supreme Court, 34
Camera, W. J., 34
Camp David Peace Accord
negotiations, 115
CE (continuing education)
programs, 78
Certification, 17
Character traits, 59
Chu, David, 56
CI activities. *See* Counterintelligence
activities
Civilian protection, 89–90
Civil Rights Act of 1991, 33, 34
Civil Service Commission, 42
Civil Service Reform Act (CSRA), 31
Clapper, James R., 56
Clarity (documentation), 66
Classified information, 20, 52, 54, 72
Client
identification of, 80, 111–113,
120, 142
organization as, 87
Clinical psychologists, 6–7, 17–18, 112
Clinical role, 112, 128
Clinton administration, 130
Colleague consultation, 63
Combatants, 89
Common sense judgment, 54–55

Competence, 16–17
for assessment and selection, 37–39
for behavioral science consultation,
99–101
for crisis negotiation consultation,
116–117
cultural, 17
establishing, 122
Ethical Standard 2.01 (Boundaries
of Competence), 37, 64,
77–78, 100–101, 116–117
for security clearance evaluation,
64–65
Standard 2.03 (Maintaining
Competence), 116–117
Conferences, 20
Confidentiality
in assessment and selection, 35,
39–41, 45
Ethical Standard 4.01 (Maintaining
Confidentiality), 39–40
Ethical Standard 4.02 (Discussing the
Limits of Confidentiality), 65
limits of, 142
in security clearance evaluation,
65–66
Confidential security clearance, 52
Conflicts of interest, 54
Consent forms, 41–42, 44–45. *See also*
Informed consent
Consultation
behavioral science. *See* Behavioral
science consultation
and counterterrorism activities,
74–75
crisis negotiation. *See* Crisis negotiation consultation
and ethical decision making, 134
with peers and colleagues, 63, 142
Consultation to interrogation, 85–99, 102
case studies, 95–101
doctrinal guidance for, 91–92
and ethical responsibilities to
society, 87–89
law relating to, 89–90
and mental health care for guards, 98
mixing behavioral health support
with, 95–96
and PENS Task Force, 141–142
and policy guidance, 92–94

Ethics Code. *See* "Ethical Principles of
    Psychologists and Code of
    Conduct"
Ethics Committee (APA), 36
Ethics of operational psychology, 13–18
    for competence, 16–17
    development of standards for, 13–14
    for informed consent, 18
    and law, 125–126
    for mixed agency, 15–16
    for multiple relationships, 17–18
    purpose of, 127
Evaluation(s). *See also* Assessment and
        selection
    for CI/CT operations, 71
    health-care, 96
    periodic, 45
    program, 42
    role of operational psychologist in, 9
    security clearance. *See* Security
        clearance evaluations
Evidence-based practice, 133
Expeditionary psychology, 7
Expertise, 3–5, 80, 92–94, 134
Expert psychologist consultants, 120

Fairness, 41, 42, 45
Federal Bureau of Investigation (FBI),
        85, 88, 107
Federal Privacy Act of 1974, 54
Fidelity, 87, 135
Financial problems, 59–60
FIS (foreign intelligence service), 72, 73
Fiske, D. W., 38
FOIA (Freedom of Information Act)
        of 1996, 41
Foreign intelligence service (FIS), 72, 73
Forensic psychology, 16, 87, 133
Freedom of Information Act (FOIA)
        of 1996, 41

Gambling addiction, 60
Gates, Robert, 56
Gelles, M. G., 16
Geneva Convention Relative to the
        Treatment of Prisoners of War, 89
Geneva Conventions
    combatants vs. noncombatants in, 36
    Common Article 3, 90
    and competence, 16

endorsement of, 91
    Protection of Civilian Persons in
        Time of War, 89–90
    and psychologist competence, 100
Greenberg, S. A., 15
Grisso, T., 88, 102
Guards
    and behavioral drift, 89
    providing mental health care for, 98
    reporting potential abuse, 98–99
Guidelines
    for crisis negotiation consultation,
        120–122
    identification and validation of, 135

Handling, 70
Hanfmann, E., 38
Health care ethics, 132
Health care providers, 121–122
Health Insurance Portability and
        Accountability Act (HIPAA), 40
High-risk operational personnel, 29, 41.
        See also Assessment and selection
HIPAA (Health Insurance Portability
        and Accountability Act), 40
Hitler, Adolf, 114
Hooding, 91
Hostage negotiation, 112–113. *See also*
        Crisis negotiation
    origins of, 107
    role of operational psychologist in,
        12–13
    training for consultation in, 116–117
Hughes, J. H., 66
Human intelligence (HUMINT)
        collection, 91. *See also* Debriefing
        operations; Interrogation
Human Intelligence Collector Operations,
        91–92
Human rights, 126, 141

IACP (International Association of
        Chiefs of Police), 43–44
Indirect assessments
    and informed consent, 18
    role of operational psychologist in,
        11–12
    standards for, 114–116
    using medical records for, 118
Industrial and organizational
        psychologists, 37

ABOUT THE EDITORS

Carrie H. Kennedy, PhD, ABPP, is a Lieutenant Commander in the Medical Service Corps of the U.S. Navy. She currently serves as an aerospace psychologist at the Naval Aerospace Medical Institute. Dr. Kennedy is the Navy's only dual-designated clinical and aerospace experimental psychologist. She serves as the Chair of the Conflict of Interest Committee for the National Academy of Neuropsychology, is the Past Chair of the American Psychological Association's Division 19 (Military Psychology) Ethics Consultation Committee, and serves as Member-at-Large of Division 19. She is the Coeditor of *Military Psychology: Clinical and Operational Applications* and *Military Neuropsychology*. She serves on the editorial boards of *Military Psychology* and *Psychological Services*.

Thomas J. Williams, PhD, is a Colonel in the Medical Service Corps of the U.S. Army. He currently serves as the Director of the Army Physical Fitness Research Institute, and Director of the Leadership Feedback Program, U.S. Army War College, Carlisle, Pennsylvania. He is a Past Chair of the Department of Psychology at the Walter Reed Army Medical Center, where he also served as the last Program Director for the Department of Defense Psychopharmacology Demonstration Project. During his time at Walter Reed, Colonel Williams also served as the strategic planner for the Walter Reed health care system and the North Atlantic Regional Medical Command. He subsequently served as the Command Psychologist, 902d Military Intelligence Group, Fort Meade, Maryland, where he supported strategic level counterintelligence and counterespionage programs worldwide. Colonel Williams has supported Special Operations Command during Operation Iraqi Freedom I and II and, most recently, served in support of Special Operations Command South during Operation Willing Spirit, which helped set the conditions for freeing the three American hostages being held by terrorists in Colombia. He has coauthored several articles and chapters focused on operational psychology. He served on the editorial board of *Military Psychology* from 2004 to 2008.